The
SORCERERS' GUIDE
TO GOOD HEALTH

This book is dedicated to
Wendy

PLEASE NOTE:

This is a collection of folk remedies, spirit rituals, and incantations practiced by traditional healers in various parts of the world, as well as their health recipes, diets, and methods of preventing illness. The incantations are often in a secret tongue, known only to the sorcerer—and presumably to the spirits with whom he wishes to communicate.

Since they represent traditional folk medicine and health practices the treatments and other health information in this book are presented only for historical and cultural interest, and *not for application to any individual case*. Persons in need of medical care should consult with their own physicians, psychiatrists—or perhaps their witch doctors—for the diagnosis and treatment of their particular ailments.

The
SORCERERS' GUIDE TO GOOD HEALTH

by Peggy Cochrane

Published by

Barricade Books Inc./Fort Lee, New Jersey

Published by

Barricade Books Inc.
1530 Palisade Ave.
Fort Lee, New Jersey 07024

Distributed by
Publishers Group West
4065 Hollis
Emeryville, CA 94608

Printed in the United States of America

Library of Congress Cataloging in Publication Data

Cochrane, Peggy.
    The sorcerers' guide to good health / Peggy Cochrane.
        p.   cm.
    ISBN 0–942637–86–0 : $14.99
    1. Folk medicine.   2. Healing—Folklore.   I. Title.
GR880.C62   1993
615.89′82—dc20   92–36262
                                                              CIP

Photographs in Africa,
    Courtesy of Scantravel Africa, Inc.,
    Tucson, Arizona. Other photographs by the author.

Contents

About the Author

Peggy Cochrane is a world traveler, a writer, a native Californian, and an A.I.A. architect. She graduated from Scripps College, in Claremont, California, with honors in architecture. She continued her studies, in both architecture and writing, at the University of Southern California, the University of California at Los Angeles, at Columbia University in New York, and in Europe. She has had her own architectural practice in Sherman Oaks, California since 1960.

Miss Cochrane first became interested in writing when she was on the staff of her school paper in college. For fifteen years she was on the editorial board of *L.A. Architect*, a publication of the American Institute of Architects. For two years, she was president of the Association of Women in Architecture, and was voted a life member. She is a member of the Union Internationale des Femmes Architectes, the Book Publicists of Southern California, the California Writers' Club, and for ten years was a member of the Dionysians, a drama group in Pasadena, where she had a play produced which won an award.

She has traveled to most of the countries of the world gathering information for her writing, and is a member of the Travelers' Century Club. She has written five books, two musicals, several plays, and numerous articles which have been published. Her biography appears in *Who's Who in the World*, *Who's Who of American Women*, and *Who's Who in the West*.

Foreword

Several years ago, Miss Cochrane visited my office for a cholera booster shot. Being a world traveler myself, I was inquisitive as to which remote country she intended to visit. She informed me that while on safari in East Africa she became interested in witch doctors and folk remedies, and was planning a trip to New Guinea to do research on a book she was writing. New Guinea was one of the few places I had never been, and it had always held a fascination for me. I asked her to send me a postcard from there, and suggested we get together upon her return to see her pictures.

A few months later, my wife and I had the good fortune to take a vacation to New Guinea during their annual Sing-Sing, where over 40,000 natives gather in their finest regalia for a week's celebration. I discovered that the natives still believed in witch doctors, and prefer to visit them before consulting with a licensed M.D.

As it happens, it was a book on folk remedies that had been in my family for several generations that inspired me to follow a medical career. I loaned this book to Miss Cochrane to help her research. After having read her manuscript, I find, to the best of my knowledge, her information is documented, and should be of enormous historical value.

Walter Peters, M.D.
Laguna Hills, California

CHAPTER ONE

Introduction

BARELY TWO HUNDRED YEARS AGO, enlightened rational-ism purged Western civilization of the supernatural. Eighteenth-century philosophers endeavored to spirit away the occult, so to speak, and succeeded to a remark-able degree. Today, with a renewed interest in a return to nature, society is experiencing a renaissance of folk remedies, faith healing, witchcraft, and psychic phe-nomena. Where people used to boast of their infections being cured by miracle drugs, they may now speak know-ingly of folk remedies they have tried. Even doctors are doing research on natural remedies as they realize the dangers and limitations of antibiotics, as well as some other modern medications.

With the growing popularity of holistic healing, which takes into account emotions as well as physical symp-toms, sorcerers' remedies are being rediscovered. Their methods, as those of more familiar "holistic" healers, en-compass all types of healing: mental, spiritual, physical, dietetic, and magical.

Many ailments are not serious enough to require the services of a physician and some ailments are psycho-somatic. Dr. David Bufford postulates that a pain-reduc-

9

ing substance in the brain is released when a patient believes he will be helped by rituals and similar practices.

Slight symptoms may indicate the beginning of a serious disease, while other symptoms, apparently more severe and painful, may be psychosomatic. Nothing annoys a busy doctor more than the hypochondriac who constantly comes running to him with illusory ailments. For this patient he may prescribe placebos, harmless pills which suggest a treatment.

Early recognition of disease is of prime importance in deciding to see a doctor. For example, patients who manage to recognize their own cancer symptoms, and see a specialist in time, are often cured. Those who rely on folk remedies should seek professional help if the ailment does not improve after folk treatment, or in any case if the ailment is more than a minor one.

Folk remedies are often useful to travelers to remote areas, and natives in the bush, who have to resort to their own treatments when the services of a physician, clinic, or hospital are unavailable. Also it is invaluable for everyone to be familiar with the rudiments of first aid, nutrition, and proper nursing care which may be acquired through community classes or a wealth of literature that is widely available.

Dr. Sheldon Neil warns of remedies, both home remedies and professional ones, which can be harmful. Chloromycetin, in excess, can cause pernicious anemia, and apple cider vinegar, a favorite folk remedy, may promote hardening of the arteries. The continued use of cortisone can be harmful, and large doses of aspirin may either be fatal or cause serious kidney damage or perforated ulcers. So knowledge and common sense should be employed in evaluating both home remedies and professional care.

For example, when a doctor advises an operation, it is wise to get a second opinion. Often surgery or amputation can be avoided with other methods of treatment. Sometimes emergency operations must be performed to save a person's life, but unless there is an emergency, nonsurgical methods could be tried first. There are reports of patients, without resort to surgery, who have been cured by holistic healing, acupuncture, or herbal remedies. All Tibetan healers oppose surgery.

A vast number of ancient remedies have been lost to medical science. Some of these are being rediscovered, and tested by teams of doctors and pharmacists some of whom visit witch doctors in remote areas. Nicole Maxwell, author of *The Witch Doctor's Apprentice*, was commissioned by a pharmaceutical company to gather herbs, and interview *brujas* in South America. In Spanish, *bruja* means witch doctor, *brujo* means sorcerer, and *cuarandero* means healer. The *brujas* along the Amazon River showed her an herb used there for birth control which apparently has no adverse side effects, as well as herbs used for burns, wounds, and schizophrenia.

Herbal remedies have been used for medical treatment by virtually every race on earth. They have been handed down from generation to generation. Included among folk remedies are a variety of strange and exotic treatments that seem to have a scientific or psychological basis. *Brujas* in Mexico, for tonsillitis, sometimes apply coyote dung directly to the tonsils. (Coyote dung contains an enzyme which generates heat.) They are fond of tequila, both internally and externally, as it is made from a cactus which reputedly has great healing power. *Brujas* in Oaxaca concoct medicine and hallucinatory drugs from wild yams and wild mushrooms.

In Hawaii, witch doctors are called *kahunas*. The *ka-*

huna anaana is a sorcerer who may use prayer to cast both good and evil spells. The *kahuna paaoao* is the pediatrician, the *kahuna haha* is the diagnostician, and the *kahuna lapaau* is an herbalist. The traditional *kahunas* wore long white robes with crowns and leis of *ti* leaves. Around their waists, they hung calabashes for mixing herbal medicines.

African *ngangas*, like the kahunas, rely on diets and herbs for many ailments. (However, it was the ancient Egyptians who discovered an herb tea for the common cold.)

Surprisingly, the folk remedy in one country is often identical with the remedy in another country thousands of miles away. (Perhaps nature *has* provided a remedy for every illness.)

Herbs have found their way into modern medicine, and are the basis of many medications. Patients who are allergic to drugs might profit from experimenting (*in consultation with their doctors*) with herbs and natural remedies, especially for minor ailments. Strong antibiotics tend to kill bacteria in the body that help to ward off disease; furthermore, their overuse builds up an immunity against them, making them ineffective, perhaps when most needed. (Some drugs in combination with herbs may be harmful, and in combination with other drugs, or with alcohol, may be fatal.)

The traditional medicine man in West Africa often has greater success than do modern doctors in treating natives. Many native patients believe they must be exorcised of evil spirits. They also feel that the isolated patient is rejected by his relatives and society, and will never recover. So in hospitals, mental institutions, and therapeutic villages, several members of the patient's family come to live with him; thereby aiding in his recovery. To Africans, family life is of prime importance. They not only worship their dead ancestors, but they believe the worst curse that can befall them is to be barren. Their practice of "togetherness," however, can pose a problem in curing infectious disease, and often leads to epidemics. Fortunately, the African *nganga* is coming to realize the validity of vaccination, personal hygiene, and the prevention of disease.

Most of the remedies in this book are reportedly considered effective by at least some traditional healers, and some of the remedies are actually soothing and pleasant.

Included here are descriptions and traditional remedies for more than 400 ailments. Although many will seem strange, even bizarre, I hope that after reading this book you will agree that many "lost" treatments are promising and should be studied for possible use in modern medical practice.

CHAPTER TWO

The Sorcerer in Modern Society

To many, the name sorcerer denotes evil, devil worship, and black magic. It's true that most sorcerers believe in the paranormal, the occult, legerdemain, and magic, but those who heal employ both black and white magic.

If the illness is diagnosed as a spell cast upon the victim by an enemy or an evil spirit, the sorcerer finds a way to break the spell by exorcism, voodoo, hex dollies, and transference. Since 75 percent of illnesses are psychosomatic or stress related, these methods can be very effective.

Psychic surgeons in the Philippines practice slight of hand by going into a trance and pretending to remove a tumor from a patient's body by reaching inside him and pulling it out. The surgeon smears a little blood, or ketchup, on his hands to make the operation appear authentic. The "tumor" which is removed may be tripe, or another part of a cow's insides. According to Dr. William Nolan, author of the book *Healing*, psychic surgery can help in the case of psychosomatic illnesses, but can be dangerous if the patient really has a malignant tumor, and is passing up the treatment he needs.

Faith healing, as practiced by many evangelists, puts the patients in the mood by playing gospel music. The minister calls the patients up to the stage one by one, and hypnotizes them. While under hypnosis they are encouraged to throw away their crutches or wheelchairs. While the patients are prancing around on the stage, thinking they are cured, they may injure themselves more.

Swamis, in India, believe in kinesiology to determine if a pill or a certain food is good for the patient. The patient holds the pill, or food, in his right hand, and extends his left hand. The swami puts his hand over the patient's left hand and applies pressure. If the patient's left hand stays in place, the pill, or food, in his right hand is good for him, but if his left hand goes down, it's bad for him, and he shouldn't take it.

Credo Mutwa, the "pope" of all Zulu shamans in South Africa, has said that his patients do not even have to tell him their symptoms: "All I have to do is look at a patient to determine his trouble."

Mr. Mutwa, a *sangoma*, was called to the profession by the spirits of his ancestors. He was apprenticed for 20 years as a *twasa* under other witch doctors to learn their secrets. He has his own herb garden, and makes herb teas for gallstones, diabetes, and many other ailments; however, for some serious diseases he might send his patients to a modern hospital.

Many *sangomas*, in South Africa, have their own muti shops where patients can buy herbs and fetishes to fill their prescriptions.

While visiting West Africa on a Traditional Medicine Tour, I witnessed a *N'Doep* ceremony in the bush country of Senegal. For eight consecutive days, the *marabout*, or sorcerer, performs a ritual, to the beat of drums, similar to the Haitian voodoo ceremony. The patient falls into a trance while his relatives dance around him. Because of their support, he feels needed, and wants to get well. On the eighth day, the *marabout* sacrifices a goat, and rubs the blood on the patient's body while exorcising the evil spirits. Costumed dancers, magicians, stilt-walkers, and fire-eaters perform, making the *N'Doep* appear like a circus.

The ju-ju man, in the Ivory Coast of Africa, believes most illnesses are caused by evil spirits, or by patients breaking a taboo. For the former, he has many ways of exorcising ghosts. His favorite method is to burn dragon's blood incense. If he wants to achieve a miracle, he burns St. Jude's incense. As spirits are thought to inhabit huts, fig trees, mountains, a fire, or the bodies of animals, he has natives build special huts for spirits to inhabit. He entices the spirits into these huts with offers of food and drink, often sacrificing a goat.

In Haiti, natives who believe in voodoo would rather visit a *houngan* (a voodoo priest) or a voodootherapist, than a licensed medical doctor. If the patient is told by the voodootherapist he will not recover, he often sinks into a depression, and death may soon follow. If however, he is informed he is going to get well, the patient often sets out on the road to recovery.

To discover if the patient will live or die, a voodootherapist goes into his private office alone, and strikes four matches in the name of the Trinity; to the left, to the right, to the back, and to the front. If the front match goes out, the patient is doomed. If all of the matches remain lighted, the therapist draws up the patient's horoscope to discover his ruling planets and his lucky and unlucky days. The voodootherapist then performs a ceremony, and a black chicken, the same sex as the patient, is sacrificed to the gods. The therapist bites off the chicken's head and sucks its blood. The patient is then required to suck the chicken's blood, and rub its feathers and blood on his forehead. After this ritual, both the patient and the therapist go into a trance, to the beat of drums, to determine the cause and the cure for the illness. Haitians, like Africans, use drumming frequencies to induce trance, visual imagery, and hallucinations.

If the patient reveals that his trouble is caused by another person, the voodootherapist advises him to make a hex dolly of his enemy. They use locks of hair, some cologne, bits of clothing, fingernail clippings, and a photograph of the person they wish to hex. They stick the doll with pins, and transfer the patient's disease to his enemy.

If the patient so desires, a voodootherapist may attempt to make the hexed person die at a certain time on a certain date. To do this he prepares an *ouanga*, a small cowhide sack containing: blood, dogs' teeth, parrots' beaks, frog bones, broken bottles, cemetery dirt, rum, and eggshells. He buries this sack near the victim's house, burns black candles, and chants this incantation: "Old master, now is the time to keep the promise you made. Curse him as I curse him and spoil him as I spoil him. By the fire at night, by the dead black hen, by the bloody throat, by the goat, by the rum on the ground, this *ouanga* be upon him. May he have no peace in bed, nor at his food, nor can he go and hide. Waste him and wear him and tear him and rot him as these rot."

As soon as these words are spoken, the victim is supposed to feel sharp pains in his body, fall into deep despair, eat nothing but dirt, and die at the prescribed time.

Instead of practicing voodootherapy, Australian aborigines may attempt to sing a person to death. The victim of this spell becomes paralyzed, and his breathing is impaired. Modern medicine cannot save him. He can only be cured by the sorcerer who dances around him waving kangaroo bones, and singing a "get-well" *icaro*.

Metaphysical sorcerers organize seances in which they become mediums to call upon the dead ancestors of the participants to solve their problems. During the seance, the house shakes, and trumpets and ghosts sail around the room. The dead ancestors appear in white gossamer robes to communicate with their decendants. The medium might also invite all of the group to gather around a wood table with their hands touching lightly on top of it. The table moves and bounces around answering questions: two bumps for "no," and three bumps for "yes." I know it works as I've been a participant, but since it is unexplained in scientific terms, it belongs to the realm of the occult.

The transference of energy is another means a sorcerer has of healing. Either by "coupling" (the laying on of hands), or by raising the "cone of power" to heal a sick person. The participants in the ceremony form a circle around the patient, where they sing and dance in unison. When they reach the zenith of their power, they are ordered by the sorcerer to stop abruptly, thereby releasing the energy cone to the patient, and burning out the diseased portions of his body.

In the medical world, there is no room for bigotry. All healers should work toward the well-being of their patients. Often, when a patient is pronounced incurable and left to die, a miracle happens and he recovers. All such "miracles"—whether in primitive or modern lands—should be investigated. There may, in fact, be not only a place, but a great future in modern society for the witch doctor and sorcerer.

CHAPTER THREE

Afflictions and Diseases with Traditional Remedies

This information is presented only because it is illustrative of the customs and practices of traditional healers in various parts of the world and for its cultural and historical interest. Do not attempt to use this information for self-diagnosis or treatment. If you need medical or health advice or treatment, consult a qualified practitioner.

Abrasions

Small scratches, scrapes, or cuts.

Treatment: Brujas in Mexico dab tequila on the wound, and leave it exposed to the air. It usually heals rapidly.

Abscesses

Symptoms: A red sore filled with pus, often on the gums.

Treatment: In ancient Egypt, shamans applied a hot baked fig directly to the abscess.

Accidents

Treatment: Vermont folk healers, as well as other healers, advise to keep calm, and keep on-lookers away. They say to look first for the three "B's": breathing, bleeding, and broken bones. They advise restoring breathing by mouth-to-mouth resuscitation, stopping any bleeding, and applying splints to broken bones before moving the patient. They recommend keeping the patient warm, and treating him for shock.

Acid Burns

Treatment: Folk practitioners in Pennsylvania apply a mixture of baking soda and water to the burn.

Acidity

Symptoms: Sour stomach, gas pains, bad breath, and indigestion.

Treatment: The traditional medicine man in Tahiti has the patient chew vanilla pods. Then he places him on a special diet (see Chapter Four: Diets), and has him drink eight glasses of water a day between meals, but no liquids with meals.

Acne

An inflammatory skin ailment common to adolescents.

Treatment: In Bolivia, teen-agers tie a red string around their necks, and go on a special diet (see Chapter Four: Diets).

New Zealand Maoris grate a raw cucumber, mix it with petroleum jelly, and apply it to the pimples.

Actinomycosis

A cattle disease peculiar to farmers; often contracted by chewing on contaminated straw.

Primary Symptoms: A hard, lumpy swelling on the lower jaw with pain, fever, vomiting, and severe emaciation.

Treatment: Sangomas in South Africa put their patients to bed, keep them warm, and feed them Zulu Brew (see Chapter Five: Health Recipes) along with a light, nourishing diet featuring sage tea several times daily. If the patient does not improve, they call a specialist to administer antibiotics.

Addison's Disease

A disease of the adrenal glands.

Primary Symptoms: Bronze skin, weight loss, hypotension, dehydration, and gastrointestinal upsets.

Treatment: Haitian *houngans* place the patient on a salty diet, and have him drink Witch Doctor's Potion (see Chapter Five: Health Recipes), and grapefruit juice.

Chinese herbalists prescribe licorice several times daily.

Adenoids

Symptoms (in children): Vacant expression, open mouth, noisy breathing, a hacking cough, a peculiar muffling of the voice, and an enlargement of the tonsils.

Treatment: Australian witch doctors steam the patient's throat by holding his mouth over the spout of a kettle of boiling water to which eucalyptus leaves have been added. Then they have him gargle hot water, with boric acid in it, every 2 hours.

Adhesions

The union of surfaces normally separated by the formation of new tissues resulting from an inflammatory process, or by operations that do not heal.

Treatment: Persian shamans apply castor oil to the adhesions, and feed the patient milk and radishes, alternated with lemons, oranges, peaches, and pomegranates.

Agranulocytosis

An acute illness sometimes due to drug hypersensitivity.

Primary Symptoms: Overpowering weakness, chills, high fever, rapid, weak pulse, sore throat, and ulcers of the oral mucosa.

Treatment: Shamans in Poland feed the patient garlic juice in hot milk, with 1 teaspoon of honey, to arrest the infection.

African *ngangas* in Uganda recommend yogurt, Shaman Surprise, Witch Doctor's Potion, and Magic Protein Potion (see Chapter Five: Health Recipes), along with strict bed rest and a diet rich in vitamin B_{12} (see Chapter Six: Vitamins and Minerals).

AIDS and ARC
(Acquired Immune Deficiency Syndrome and AIDS Related Complex)

Symptoms: Persistent swollen glands in the neck, armpits, or groin, tiredness or fatigue, sudden weight loss, night sweats, fever or chills, diarrhea lasting more than two weeks, a dry cough with shortness of breath, white spots in the mouth, new flat or raised blotches or bumps that are discolored from the surrounding skin appear on or under the skin, mouth, or eyelids; bleeding gums, and susceptibility to other diseases particularly cancer and pneumonia. Symptoms may not appear for six years.

Causes: Having sex with infected persons, using dirty hypodermic needles, receiving contaminated blood transfusions, and infected mothers passing on the disease to their babies.

Prevention: People should only have sex with one partner; or those who "swing" should wear condoms (even though they are only 75 percent safe). Drug users should use only sterile or disposable needles, or give up their habit. Infected mothers should not nurse their babies, and all blood transfusions should be tested for AIDS, ARC, and HIV.

Treatment: Ngangas in Zaire think it came from the blood of the green monkey. A quack witch doctor drew out the blood of the green monkey, and mixed it with the blood of a bride and groom in a wedding ceremony. During this secret ritual, he made an incision in the stomachs of both the bride and groom, mixing the three blood types into them. For that reason, many *ngangas* believe that AIDS should first be treated with blood purifiers. They suggest a patient eat garlic, and sip two cups of sassafras tea daily. They put him on the Diet for Assimilation (Poor) (see Chapter Four: Diets), add royal jelly and bee pollen to his cereal, and since the disease is fatal, send him to a therapeutic village for treatment. While the patient is at the village, the patient's family visit him to attend to his diet and needs. The *nganga* attempts to exorcise the evil spirits from the patient's body, and hangs a "hag stone" (a stone with a hole in it) over his bed. He arranges parties and ceremonies for him, thereby relieving his stress and making him laugh. In Africa, the patient feels loved, needed, and wanted.

The West African ju-ju man suggests AIDS patients press a ruby hard between their hands to send healing energy through the body.

Marabouts, in Senegal, arrange a *N'Doep* ceremony for the patient.

Houngans, in Haiti, attempt to cure patients in Voodoo ceremonies.

In Wales and Guernsey, there is a cult of white witches called *Wicca* who practice the "cone of power" ceremony for patients with incurable diseases.

Airsickness

Prevention: Mexican *brujas* suggest sucking on hard candies.

Treatment: Hawaiian *kahunas* recommended drinking a cup of ginger tea, and placing a paper sack over the chest next to the skin.

Alcoholism

Treatment: Maoris in New Zealand have the patient eat honey, and substitute Kiwi Pick-Me-Ups and Rookery Revivers (see Chapter Five: Health Recipes) for alcoholic beverages.

Alkali Burns

Treatment: For burns caused by strong alkalis, such as lye or ammonia, New England folk practitioners advise flooding the burn with vinegar.

Alkalinity

Symptoms: Burping caused by taking bicarbonate of soda for acid stomach, or by an alkaline imbalance in the system.

Treatment: South American *curanderos* in Chile have their patients sip white wine or cold champagne.

Mexican *brujas* recommend well-balanced meals containing citrus fruit.

Allergies

Hypersensitivity to certain plants, materials, smoke, animals, foods, or even to other people.

Primary Symptoms: Headache, sneezing, breaking out in a rash, running nose, and watering and itching eyes.

Treatment: Folk practitioners in Vermont feed their patients 2 teaspoons honey in 2 teaspoons vinegar with a half glass of water, before breakfast and at bedtime.

Alzheimer's Disease

Symptoms: Memory loss, change in personality, confusion, irritability, inability to concentrate or learn new things, inability to care for one's self, eventually leading to death.

Causes: A degeneration of the blood vessels of the brain causing brain shrinkage, hardening of the arteries, a blow to the head, being hypnotized or mesmerized.

Prevention: Pennsylvania folk healers say don't eat anything, or store any food or drink, in aluminum pans or cans, don't store or cook acidic or salty foods in aluminum foil, and don't use deodorants containing aluminum. They suggest cutting down on smoking, or don't smoke, and be active socially—especially playing bridge which requires concentration.

Treatment: Hopi Indian medicine men construct amulets made from petrified wood which they hang around patients' necks.

Mexican *brujas* put their patients on a special diet (see Chapter Four: Diets).

Amenorrhea

Cessation or absence of the menses. After age 50, it's usually due to menopause.

Treatment: Russian shamans have the patient drink beet syrup, or tansy tea.

In India, gurus prescribe hot gin with quinine in it.

Midwives in Russia and India warn that these remedies should not be taken in the case of pregnancy as they could cause miscarriage.

Anemia

Primary Symptoms: The blood is light red or orange, and the patient feels weak and loses weight.

Prevention: African Masais in Tanzania drink cow's blood in milk.

Treatment: South African *sangomas* prescribe deer's blood in red wine, and put the patient on a special diet (see Chapter Four: Diets).

Aneurysm

A serious, often fatal, condition characterized by an abnormal dilation of a blood vessel, usually an artery.

Treatment: English folk practitioners apply a comfrey poultice.

Angina Pectoris

Pain in the chest caused by insufficient blood supply to the heart.

Treatment: Bavarian gypsies prescribe 1/2 teaspoon cayenne pepper in a cup of water, and hawthorn berries. They advise patients to eat sesame seeds, keep their weight down, and avoid sudden, strenuous exercise.

Ant Bites

Treatment: Mexican *brujas* apply a solution of baking soda and water to the bites after brushing them with a cow tail.

Anthrax

Causes: Contact with infected animals, or eating infected meat.

Primary Symptoms: Lesions and pustules on the face, neck, arms, and hands. They have a brown center with a bright red ring. On the second day, vestules develop at the periphery of the pustule. These are bluish red and discharge a fluid. Also, there is headache, nausea, vomiting, joint pains, malaise, chills, and fever.

Treatment: In Poland, shamans feed the patient 1 tablespoon of raw potato juice every 2 hours, and have him maintain strict bed rest. If he does not improve, they call a specialist as the disease is often fatal.

Appendicitis

Primary Symptoms: Sharp pain in the right side followed by constipation.

Treatment: Russian shamans wring out a cloth in hot water with 8 drops of turpentine, and place it on the painful area. They advise not giving any purgatives because of possible rupture. If possible, they send the patient to a hospital.

In Oaxaca, Mexican *brujas* make an extract of wild yams, and pour 1 teaspoon in a glass of water, giving 1 teaspoon every half hour.

Arteriosclerosis
(Hardening of the Arteries)

Primary Symptoms: Loss of appetite, headache, coldness of the hands and feet, absentmindedness, ringing in the ears, and weakness. This ailment is more common to those past middle age.

Prevention: Healers in Sicily advise older people to eat

one raw bud of garlic daily, and avoid drinking apple cider vinegar.

Hawaiian *kahunas* recommend fresh pineapple twice daily.

Treatment: In New England, to increase blood circulation, folk practitioners have patients eat pure oatmeal with cream, honey, and bananas. Then, several times daily, they have patients drink the water in which the oatmeal has been boiled.

Arthritis

Primary Symptoms: Discomfort and swelling in the joints, persistent pain and stiffness on rising, tingling sensations in the fingertips, hands, and feet; unexplained weight loss, and fatigue. In advanced cases, there may be joint damage and crippling.

Treatment: Hawaiian *kahunas* massage the patient's joints with coconut oil or cold pressed peanut oil.

Sangomas in South Africa advise chewing wheatgrass sprouts.

Marabouts in Senagal place a poultice of live black ants (a prime source of formic acid) on the affected area.

Polish shamans suggest patients carry a wild chestnut in their pocket.

Mexican *brujas* make a liniment out of 1/2 cup each of ruta herb, fresh rosemary, pepper tree leaves and bark, with 1 mashed avocado seed in 1/2 gallon of rubbing alcohol. They let this stand for a couple of days until it turns black, and then rub it on the painful areas.

Russian healers boil fresh birch leaves for 30 minutes (2 pounds in 2 gallons of water), and add them to the patient's bath. Then they have him drink 2 cups of pleurisy tea.

New Zealand Maoris recommend eating sea mussels called *perna.*

Hungarian gypsies advise patients to take a hot Jacuzzi bath with 1/2 cup of epsom salts added. Then they put him on a special diet (see Chapter Four: Diets).

Asphyxiation

Loss of consciousness due to noxious vapors
Treatment: Folk healers in Wales move the patient to the open air, dash cold water in his face, and rub vinegar around his nostrils. When he revives, they feed him lemonade slowly.

Assimilation (Poor)

Symptoms: Loss of weight and a pasty complexion. The patient is extremely nervous, and has nerve pains below the shoulder blade on the right side of the spine.
Treatment: Marabouts in Senegal place an amulet of jasper around the patient's neck and have him drink saffron in water (1 teaspoon to 1 gallon of water) several times daily. Then they put him on a special diet (see Chapter Four: Diets).

Asthma

A disorder of the upper respiratory tract.
Symptoms: Wheezing, coughing, and choking.
Treatment: Cherokee Indian medicine men have the patient smoke cigarettes made out of dried stramonium leaves. Then they pour apple brandy over rock candy, and feed it to him slowly.
Russian shamans prescribe fox's liver in red wine.

Athlete's Foot

Symptoms: Peeling of skin and crustations between the toes.
Treatment: Greek healers have patients soak their feet

in salt water and dust them with cornstarch. Then they put patients on a special diet (see Chapter Four: Diets) and have them wear well-ventilated shoes.

Houngans in Haiti rub the patient's toes with lemon and salt, after which he soaks the patient's feet in household bleach.

Atrophy

Symptoms: Wasting away of the flesh, tissue, or organ sometimes characterized by a withered arm or clubfoot. Babies may fail to sit or stand, and the head control may be poor. Numbness and tingling in the legs, and a froglike posture are additional manifestations.

Treatment: In Togo, ju-ju men place a necklace of frog bones around the patient's neck, and have him drink lots of citrus fruit juice.

Backache

Treatment: Kahunas in Hawaii have the patient sit in a bathtub and let hot water run continuously over a pile of ordinary stones. They rub his back with warm eucalyptus oil, and feed him nettle tea several times daily. If he is suffering from a slipped disc, they apply papaya to the painful area.

For serious back pain the Chinese prescribe acupuncture.

Baldness
(Alopecia)

Treatment: In Russia, shamans feed the patient seaweed, apply crude oil shampoo to his scalp, followed by massage, and rub his head with garlic juice twice daily. Every twelve days after that, they rub his head with lard, and feed him garlic.

Barber's Itch

A contagious parasitic affliction attacking the hair and follicles of the beard.

Treatment: Turkish shamans shave off the beard and apply toothpaste, or an ointment of 4 ounces vaseline, 2 ounces sulphur, and 2 drams ammoniac, to the sores.

Bedbugs

Treatment: Persian shamans pour kerosene around the bed and in cracks in the floor, and apply a paste of baking soda and water to the bites.

Bedsores

Treatment: Ju-ju men in West Africa bathe the patient with 2 teaspoons of brandy in a wine glass of hot water.

Bed-Wetting
(Enuresis)

Treatment: New England folk practitioners feed the patient 1 teaspoon of honey before bedtime. This treatment is not used for babies.

Bee Stings

Treatment: Turkish shamans apply wet tobacco to the sting.

Brujas in Mexico pick three leaves from three different trees, and place them on the victim's head under his hat.

Hawaiian *kahunas* place papaya leaves on the sting.

Beriberi

Primary Symptoms: Extreme weakness, pallid skin, malnutrition, and loss of weight; often fatal.

Treatment: Gurus in India advise patients to eat well-balanced meals containing whole grain cereals, cracked wheat bread, tomatoes, green vegetables, nuts, and milk; and avoid eating polished rice.

Bilious Fever

Fever sometimes contracted from tick bites.

Primary Symptoms: Languor, alternate fits of heat and cold, severe pains in the head and back, intense heat over the whole body, thirst, white tongue, yellow eyes and skin, nausea, and vomiting of bilious matter.

Treatment: Curanderos in Bolivia take a tumbler 2/3 full of cold water, and add to it 10 drops tincture of aconite root (monkshood). Because this herb is poisonous, they limit the dose to 1 teaspoon every half hour when fever is highest, and every hour during the remission for a few days, all under their supervision.

Biliousness

Symptoms: Languor, dull headache, fullness, and slight yellowness of the eyes and skin.

Treatment: Navajo Indian medicine men have their patients eat lemons, and go on a special diet (see Chapter Four: Diets).

Birth Control

African women in Zimbabwe wear around their waists a charm made from the roots of the *mbinjiri* tree.

Women in India mix the juice of the *butea monsperma* flower with rabbit's blood and drink this, as they believe it will destroy fertility forever.

In South America along the Amazon River women take the root of the *piripiri* plant, grind it up, mix it with water, and drink a cup of it, supposing it to destroy fertility for six or seven years. To restore fertility, they drink a cup of tea made from the leaves of the *yerba de fertilidad* plant, while singing a special *icaro*.

Bleeding

Treatment: Hungarian gypsies used to apply sugar to wounds to stop bleeding, but now they apply pressure to the wound first to stop the bleeding, and then apply sugar several hours later to ward off infection, and aid healing.

During the Dark Ages in Europe, sorcerers applied cobwebs to wounds to stop bleeding. Dirty wounds were covered with a poultice of bread and lukewarm water to promote bleeding.

Navajo Indian medicine men apply a poultice of woundwort, or wood sage, to bleeding wounds.

Curanderos in Peru apply the herb *sangre de grado* to stop bleeding; for internal bleeding, they make a tea of the herb for the patient to drink.

Folk practitioners in Yugoslavia apply 1 teaspoon of alum in a cup of water to bleeding wounds.

Blisters

Symptoms: Painful collections of fluid under the skin.

Prevention: Spanish gypsies rub soap on stockings and gloves.

Treatment: Persian shamans apply camphorated oil to blisters.

Blood Poisoning
(Septicemia or Pyemia)

Primary Symptoms: A very serious, often fatal, condition characterized by small boils on certain parts of the body, pain, alternating fever and chills, throbbing, swelling and redness around the wound, reddish streaks up the arm or leg from the wound, sweating, and diarrhea.

Treatment: Navajo Indian medicine men take the juice of 1/2 lemon, add 1 teaspoon sugar and 1/2 teaspoon hot water. They suppose that the patient is helped by a dose of this mixture every 30 minutes for the first 3 hours, and then every 2 hours.

Blood Pressure (High)
(Hypertension)

Primary Symptoms: Headache, dizziness, and swollen ankles; however, often there are no symptoms. Hypertension can lead to strokes and heart attacks.

Treatment: Vermont folk practitioners recommend plenty of bed rest, moderate exercise, a low-salt diet (see Chapter Four: Diets), cold showers, and a vacation to relieve stress.

Hawaiian *kahunas* have patients eat horseradish, and garlic, and drink the fermented sap of the coconut, and red clover tea.

Blood Pressure (Low)

Treatment: Cherokee Indian medicine men feed patients goldenseal tea with a dash of red pepper, and put them on a special diet (see Chapter Four: Diets), with moderate exercise in fresh air.

Boils

A painful pus-producing inflammation of the skin.

Treatment: Hungarian gypsies cover the boil with the membrane from inside an egg shell, and feed the patient one cup of sassafras tea.

Breathing Disorders

Treatment: New England folk healers have their patients chew honeycomb.

Russian shamans prescribe eating the roasted liver of a fox.

Bright's Disease

Primary Symptoms: A kidney disease characterized by dropsy of the body, hands, and feet; swollen and puffy face, a dry harsh skin, great thirst, and a frequent desire to pass water.

Prevention: New England folk practioners advise not eating any food cooked in aluminum pans.

Treatment: Australian shamans sponge the patient's spine with cold water and put him on a low-salt diet (see Chapter Four: Diets). Then they have him take a hot bath, with a few drops of eucalyptus oil added, put him to bed, and feed him copious amounts of sage tea alternated with clove tea.

Bronchitis

Inflammation of the bronchial tubes.

Primary Symptoms: Sore throat, and coughing. Sometimes there is fever, weakness, and loss of appetite.

Treatment: Hungarian gypsies advise patients to stop smoking, and to go to bed. They boil lemon juice and rinds, and add honey to make a cough syrup. They also apply a poultice of fried onions to the chest.

Chinese herbalists prescribe licorice and grapefruit juice.

Bruises

Injuries which don't break the skin, but often turn purple or black and blue.

Treatment: Folk healers in Singapore apply hot water to the bruise, and use sun, or sunlamp treatment, along with vitamin E, both externally and internally.

Bubonic Plague

A serious, often fatal, disease caused by the bites, or flea bites, of infected rodents.

Primary Symptoms: Headache, high fever, delirium, stiff joints, swollen glands in groin and armpits, black tongue, and foul breath.

Prevention: Vaccination is the most effective and is encouraged by many witch doctors. Natives in Uganda wear an amulet containing a piece of red wool, a lion's claw, and a hazelnut to ward off the disease.

Treatment: Vermont folk healers sponge the patient with vinegar, and call a medical specialist.

Buerger's Disease

Inflammation of the lining of the blood vessels forming blood clots.

Primary Symptoms: Coldness, numbness, tingling, or burning pains in the afflicted limb (usually the leg). If the disease goes untreated, gangrene may develop.

Treatment: Bavarian gypsies massage the patient's legs with rubbing alcohol, and keep his feet warm and dry. They advise strict bed rest, and a well-balanced diet with raw onions, green vegetables, and royal jelly (the food of queen bees).

Bullet Wounds

In China, herbalists clean the wound with alcohol and apply an elm poultice before having a surgeon remove the bullet. Later they feed the patient a cup of camomile tea.

Bunions

Symptoms: A painful swelling on the foot.

Treatment: Ngangas in The Gambia apply a poultice of slippery elm.

Burns

Symptoms: Burns are classified into three categories:
  1) First degree burns: reddening of the skin.

2) Second degree burns: blistering.
3) Third degree burns: charring.

Treatment: For first degree burns, Vermont folk healers apply cold tea, and for second degree burns, they apply honey. For third degree burns, if the arms and legs are burned, they elevate the afflicted limbs above the head, and feed the patient 1 teaspoon of salt, and 1/2 teaspoon of baking soda to a quart of water, just a sip at a time, before moving him to a hospital.

For all burns, especially x-ray burns, Mexican *brujas* apply the juice and pulp of the aloe vera plant.

Curanderos in Peru apply the leaves of the *hooweeyo* plant.

Bursitis
(Tennis Elbow)

Symptoms: Severe stiffness and pain in the arm or elbow.

Treatment: Australian shamans soak the arm in hot water with epsom salts, and then massage it with olive oil and salt.

Caisson Disease
(The Bends)

This disease is common to miners and divers who are subject to rapid reduction of air pressure, and is caused by surfacing too quickly.

Primary Symptoms: Pain in the legs or abdomen, itching, dizziness and staggers, paralysis of the face, arms, and legs on one side of the body, and pressure in the eardrums.

Treatment: New Zealand Maoris advise to recompress the worker by putting him back into the ocean, or mine, and then bring him to the surface very slowly.

Calluses

Symptoms: Painful scales on the balls of the foot.

Treatment: New England folk practitioners apply castor oil nightly to the callus.

Cancer
(Carcinoma)

Symptoms: According to the American Cancer Society:
1) A sore that does not heal within two weeks.
2) Any irregular lump, or soreness in any part of the body.
3) Any irregular, unusual, or unexplained bleeding or discharge from any part of the body.
4) Any wart or mole that begins to change rapidly in size or color.
5) A persistent cough or hoarseness (especially with spitting of blood, or trouble in swallowing).
6) Recurrent or continuous indigestion.
7) Any abrupt change in bowel habits.
8) Unexplained general weakness and loss of weight.
9) Any change in color of skin, such as increasing paleness and grayness.
10) Any headache that persists and increases.

Prevention: Vermont folk healers advise not to cook food in aluminum pans, avoid smoking, and eat two almonds per day.

Treatment: South African *sangomas* have their patients, with cancer symptoms, see a cancer specialist as soon as possible. Then they put them on a special diet (see Chapter Four: Diets).

Cherokee Indian medicine men apply a comfrey poultice to the cancerous area, and have the patient drink chaparral tea.

Cancer specialists in Mexico concoct a serum from apricots called laetrile.

Hawaiian *kahunas* have their patients eat papaya seeds.

Some New Guinea witch doctors introduce their patients to malaria mosquitoes as they think a high fever will arrest the cancer.

For skin cancer, *brujas* in Oaxaca, Mexico apply the green flesh of the pipe organ cactus for ten days.

Persian shamans, for throat cancer, feed their patients tea made from violet flowers, and put violet poultices on their throats.

Canker Sores

Symptoms: Small white sores in the mouth.

Treatment: Folk practitioners in New England recommend that patients drink a glass of tomato juice.

Carbuncle

Symptoms: An infection of deeper layers of the skin, usually appearing on the neck or back, like a large boil.

Treatment: Krou witch doctors in Thailand apply a poultice of poppy leaves steeped in flaxseed meal.

Carsickness

Symptoms: Nausea and vomiting due to the motion of riding in a car.

Treatment: Shamans in Afghanistan sometimes take sheets of writing paper, glue them together, and place them on the patient's skin, under his clothes.

Catalepsy

Primary Symptoms: Loss of consciousness with rigidity. The legs may be bent, but stay in the position in which they are placed, no matter how awkward.

Treatment: *Ngangas* in Zimbabwe mash plantain leaves and feed the patient the juice, 1 teaspoon twice daily.

Catarrh

Symptoms: Red eyes, fullness and heat in the nostrils, and a thin fluid running from the nose.

Treatment: Curanderos in Peru take 1/2 pint of llama's milk, add 1/4 teaspoon salt, and have the patient snuff a little into each nostril three times daily until recovered.

Centipede Bite

A poisonous "insect," with many legs, found in desert areas.

Treatment: Navajo Indian medicine men tie a tourniquet above the wound for a few minutes, cut the wound, suction out some blood, and then apply a few drops of undiluted ammonia.

Chapped Hands

Causes: Hands, face, lips, elbows, and heels often become chapped when exposed to dry weather.

Treatment: Vermont folk healers wash the afflicted part with vinegar, and apply equal parts of honey and petroleum jelly.

Chest Colds

Symptoms: Congestion and pain in the chest.

Treatment: Folk healers in England apply a Mustard Plaster (see Chapter Five: Health Recipes) to the patient's chest.

Chest Pains

Treatment: Hungarian gypsies have the patient go to bed, and take 1 teaspoon cayenne pepper in water. Then they rub his chest with warm camphorated oil several times daily.

In Hawaii, the *kahuna lapaau* applies papaya to the chest overnight, but if this doesn't relieve the pain, he calls a specialist, either a *kahuna haha* or a licensed physician, as it could mean a heart condition or tuberculosis.

Chickenpox

Primary Symptoms: A red rash over the body and scalp.
Treatment: Mexican *brujas* apply cold cream mixed with baking soda to prevent itching. They include tomatoes, oranges, and limes in the patient's diet, and give him equal amounts of sulphur and cream of tartar in water—1 teaspoon daily.

Chilblain

Symptoms: Painful, inflammatory swelling of deep purple color affecting the extremities of the body in cold weather.
Treatment: Shamans in Iran apply equal parts of Lime Water (see Chapter Five: Health Recipes), and olive oil to the swelling.

Choking

Treatment: Maoris in New Zealand try to have the patient eat a piece of dry bread while they chant: *"Takoto i waho."*

Cholecystitis

An inflammation of the gallbladder.
Primary Symptoms: Colic, nausea, vomiting, and biliousness.
Treatment: Spanish gypsies prescribe orange juice and baked potato peelings.

Cholera

A contagious, often fatal, disease common to Asia and the Middle East. The primary source of infection is in the excreta of infected victims. The disease is spread through contact with these discharges which are carried by water, raw food, and flies.

Symptoms: In mild cases diarrhea may be the only symptom; however, in severe cases there is profuse diarrhea, prostration, tremors, vomiting, dizziness, faintness, bloody discharges, burning heat at the stomach, coldness and dampness of the body, cold tongue and breath, great dehydration with thirst, sunken eyes with dark circles under them, a peculiar body odor, and stomach cramps.

Prevention: Vaccination is good for six months, but is only 50% effective.

Treatment: Folk healers in Afghanistan apply Mustard Plasters (see Chapter Five: Health Recipes) to the patient's feet, feed him brandy in water, and later give him 1/2 teaspoon cayenne pepper in tea as his regular drink. They put him to bed, and try to find a doctor who makes house calls.

Cholera Infantum

Symptoms: A disease common to children under 3 years of age characterized by vomiting and diarrhea.

Treatment: An ancient Roman remedy was to peel and mash ripe tomatoes, add sugar, and give 1 teaspoonful every 1/2 hour until relieved, and then every 2 or 3 hours.

Chorea
(St. Vitus' Dance)

Symptoms: This disease is quite common to children, and is characterized by difficulty in walking and talking, and jerking movements.

Treatment: Guerisseurs in West Africa take the child to the beach for swimming and sea air.

In Tibet, which is landlocked, sorcerers burn St. Rita's incense, and have patients drink Indian hemp root tea.

Cirrhosis of the Liver

Causes: This often fatal disease may be caused by alcoholism, gallstones, or a chronic infection.

Primary Symptoms: The hardening of the liver with a bacterial infection causing abscesses on the liver. It is characterized by gastrointestinal disturbances, jaundice, foul breath, and weight loss.

Treatment: Maoris in New Zealand feed patients well-balanced meals, Kiwi Pick-Me-Ups (see Chapter Five: Health Recipes) and groelandica tea, with a complete abstinence from alcoholic beverages. They may also call a specialist.

Cold Feet

Treatment: Shamans in Romania have the patient wear a wool sock on one foot and a cotton sock on the other foot, alternating them every day. They also have the patient plunge his feet first into a pail of hot water and then into a pail of cold water, repeating three or four times, then rub his feet briskly with a rough towel.

Colds

Primary Symptoms: Sneezing and running of the nose.

Treatment: Sangomas in South Africa have their patients avoid rich foods and dairy products, advising them instead to drink copious amounts of water between meals, citrus fruit juice, and rose hips tea.

The New England folk practitioner bundles his patient up in a blanket, soaks his feet in hot water, and has him drink three or four cups of hot port wine, with lemon and cloves, before putting him to bed.

English folk healers have the patient drink 1 teaspoon of baking soda with the juice of 1/2 lemon in a glass of cold water every 3 hours.

Hawaiian *kahunas* have their patients gargle sea water.

Chinese herbalists make a soup of garlic, ginger, and watercress for their patients to drink.

Ancient Egyptian medical men prescribed fenugreek tea, three times daily.

Cold Sores
(Herpes Simplex)

Contagious sores on the lip, sometimes triggered by too much sun, or susceptibility to colds.

Treatment: Curanderos along the Amazon River apply wax from the patient's ear to the sore.

Colic

Symptoms: This disease is quite common to infants, and is characterized by severe twisting, gripping pains in the abdomen, but no fever. The baby doubles himself up, lies on his stomach, rolls on the floor, and starts to cry, wreathing in agony.

Treatment: Australian witch doctors feed the baby a cup of hot milk with 2 teaspoons of sugar in it.

Turkish shamans blow tobacco smoke on the soles of the baby's feet.

Colitis

Inflammation of the colon, often due to stress and nervousness.

Primary Symptoms: Acute irritation followed by either constipation or diarrhea, and colicky pain. In ulcerative colitis, there may be blood in the stool, dysentery, and fever.

Treatment: Shamans in Poland have their patients drink warm milk with garlic and honey in it every night before bedtime.

Hawaiian *kahunas* put their patients on a s
(see Chapter: Diets), and have them take hot s...
with sea salt.

Cherokee Indian medicine men prescribe goldenseal
tea twice daily.

Concussion of the Brain

Cerebral concussion usually caused by a severe blow to
the head.

Primary Symptoms: Insensibility, pale face, and cold
extremities.

Treatment: An ancient Egyptian remedy was to moisten
the patient's tongue with a few drops of tincture of arnica
(a poisonous herb) every hour the first day.

Vermont folk practitioners recommend the patient be
kept quiet, and in a warm bed for two or three weeks.
They bathe his head with vinegar, and if he does not
improve, they call a specialist.

Constipation

The retention of solid waste material in the intestines,
causing headaches and gas pains.

Treatment: Hawaiian *kahunas* put their patients on a
special diet (see Chapter Four: Diets), have them chew
hibiscus blossoms, and drink coconut water, and plantain
tea.

In both Egypt and China, folk practitioners feed their
patients licorice.

English folk healers prescribe senna tea twice daily.

Convulsions

Symptoms: Twitching of the face muscles, rolling of the
eyes, and irregularity of breathing. Severe cases are

characterized by sudden loss of sensibility, violent move-ments of arms, legs, and head, frothing of the mouth, and clenching of the hands.

Treatment: Shamans in Russia put a stick in the patient's mouth, and apply spirits of turpentine to the back of his neck.

Persian witch doctors bathe the patient's face with salt water, and when he comes to, feed him a little salt water.

Coral Cuts

Treatment: In Tahiti, the traditional healer sprinkles the cuts with lime juice.

Corns

Small, hard, painful lumps on the toes, often due to wearing ill-fitting shoes.

Treatment: Kahunas in Hawaii have their patients go barefoot, and apply papaya juice to the corn.

African *ngangas* in Kenya apply castor oil, or corn oil, to the lump.

Coughs

Treatment: Along the Amazon River, in Colombia, *brujas* place a string of corn cobs around the patient's neck.

Irish folk healers sprinkle raw onions with brown sugar, let them stand overnight, and add whiskey to the juice for the patient to drink.

Cramps

A spasmodic contraction of muscles causing stiffness and pain.

Treatment: Australian lifeguards suggest victims of leg cramp move up and down slowly on the balls of their feet.

Druid sorcerers in Ireland tie an eel's skin around the knee.

Croup

Primary Symptoms: A harsh, brassy cough with difficult respiration, and characterized by a wheezing sound. It occurs mostly in babies and young children.

Prevention: In ancient Egypt, shamans placed a black cotton thread around the child's neck.

Treatment: Folk healers in England put a piece of bacon on the child's throat, bundle him in a blanket, and hold him in a steamy bathroom.

Cushing's Syndrome

Primary Symptoms: This is a rare disease particular mostly to females. It is characterized by obesity (a "buffalo" type, confined to the face and trunk, with protruding abdomen, and a pad of fat on the back of the neck), slender extremities, easy bruising, acne, muscle weakness, hypertension, and diabetes.

Treatment: Chinese herbalists advise a low-salt diet (see Chapter Four: Diets), and licorice; however, since this disease is often fatal, they might call a Western doctor for his opinion.

Cystic Fibrosis

An inherited disease of the glands affecting the pancreas, respiratory system, and sweat glands, occurring mostly in infants and children.

Primary Symptoms: Coughing, loss of weight, a barrel-like chest, susceptibility to heat prostration, sweating, but no fever.

Treatment: Houngans in Haiti feed their patients mashed bananas.

Cystitis

Inflammation of the bladder.

Symptoms: A frequent urge to pass water, often with pus. Painful spasms radiating into the upper parts of the body. Low fever, rapid pulse, and chills also may be present.

Treatment: Ngangas in Uganda give patients tea made from yellow wax bean pods, and put them on a special diet (see Chapter Four: Diets).

Dandruff

Symptoms: Flaky white particles on the scalp, often leading to falling hair.

Treatment: Vermont folk practitioners advise washing hair often with a dandruff remover shampoo, and going on a special diet (see Chapter Four: Diets).

In Russia, shamans rub warm corn oil generously into the patient's scalp, and then tie a towel, wrung out in hot water, on his head, while feeding him 1 teaspoon of corn oil.

Deafness

Total or partial loss of hearing due to cold, inflammation of the internal ear, or the collection of wax in the ear. It can also be caused by loud noise.

Treatment: Shamans in Sicily stew garlic in olive oil, press and strain it. Then they apply a few drops of the juice each day with a warm teaspoon, and stop the ear with cotton.

Delirium Tremens

A psychic disorder usually occurring during withdrawal from alcohol by habitual users.

Symptoms: Trembling of the tongue, and hallucinations, as of "pink elephants" or snakes.

Treatment: Folk healers in Finland advise their patients to take a sauna bath for 30 minutes, and then go to bed. They give him 2 tablespoons of brandy in water every 2 hours, and when he is better, feed him honey, but no more liquor.

Ju-ju men on the Ivory Coast of Africa exorcise the hallucinations by burning black candles, shaking rattles, and dancing around the patient, while chanting an incantation.

Marabouts in Senegal perform a *N'Doep* ceremony.

Dengue Fever

A virus infection transmitted by mosquitoes in hot, humid weather. This disease rarely lasts longer than seven days, but may return from time to time.

Symptoms: Headache, extreme exhaustion, intense pain in the back, pain behind the eyes, high fever (sometimes 106°F.), a pale pink, spotty rash, and a flushed face.

Treatment: In Hawaii, *kahunas* place an ice pack on the patient's head, and sponge his face with cold water with a few drops of eucalyptus oil added. Then they have him drink several cups of *ti* leaf tea, and put him on a diet of fruit juice, and homemade chicken soup until recovered.

Dermatitis
(Skin Fungus or Jungle Rot)

An inflammation of the skin often caused by a hot, humid climate, or an allergy.

Treatment: Haitian *houngans* sponge the skin with vinegar and apply cold cream. If the weather is hot and humid, they advise patients to sleep in air-conditioned rooms.

Mexican *brujas* mash two sow bugs, and apply them to the skin.

Devil's Grip

Symptoms: Extremely sharp spasms of pain in the chest wall. Coughing, sneezing, and deep breathing aggravate the pain. Fever is usually present. This disease occurs mostly in warm weather among children and teen-agers. Diagnosis is important, as symptoms may indicate other conditions.

Treatment: Healers in Israel apply hot oatmeal poultices to the patient's chest, and feed him homemade chicken soup.

Diabetes

Symptoms: It is characterized by immoderate flow of urine containing a large amount of sugar. At times the patient feels faint, his mouth is dry and parched, and his appetite is craving.

Treatment: Folk healers in Sicily feed the patient 2 buds of garlic, and then put him on a special diet (see Chapter Four: Diets). If possible, they call a specialist as the disease is often fatal.

In Ghana, the *nganga* feeds his patients bean skin tea several times daily, and gives each an amulet containing a pearl.

Diarrhea

Symptoms: Frequent looseness of the bowels.

Treatment: Shamans in the Balkan countries advise patients to drink peppermint tea and eat blackberries.

Diphtheria

Primary Symptoms: Chills, sore throat, difficulty in swallowing, hoarseness, extreme prostration, body odor, bad breath, fever drowsiness, delirium, and runny nose.

Prevention: Vaccination.

Treatment: Healers in Ireland place a pan of chopped raw onions in the sickroom to prevent contagion. Then they have the patient gargle lemon juice and water every 2 hours with 1/2 teaspoonful swallowed.

Diverticulitis

Primary Symptoms: Pain in the left lower abdomen, bloating, and alternating constipation and diarrhea due to inflammation of small pockets in the colon. Sometimes there is malaise, chills, fever, and hemorrhaging.

Treatment: English folk healers apply heat locally, and put the patient on a low-residue diet (see Chapter Four: Diets).

Shamans in Russia give the patient 8 drops of belladonna tincture (the same poisonous compound used much in 19th century medicine) in water before each meal, and if bleeding occurs, feed him shepherd's purse tea several times daily.

Dizziness

Symptoms: A sensation of "swimming" in the head. It is often the symptom of eyestrain, ear trouble, or a disease.

Treatment: West African *guerisseurs* have the patient lie down with head raised, and feed him hot tea with lemon and cloves, just a sip at a time.

Dropsy

Symptoms: Extreme swelling throughout the body, usually caused by the accumulation of water due to the degeneration of the kidneys.

Treatment: Navajo Indian medicine men have their patients eat parsley (which has been chopped very fine), and peeled lemons sprinkled with sugar several times daily.

Drowning

Treatment: Yugoslavian gypsies have been known to hold the victim upside down over the smoke of a fire until he sneezes, and then give him a shot of brandy.

Dum Dum Fever
(Kala-Azar)

This is a rural disease prevalent in Egypt, China, Ghana, Manchuria, and Pakistan. It is caused by sandfly bites, usually in the early evening.

Primary Symptoms: Fever, chills, profuse sweating, pains in the muscles, bones, and joints; dizziness, congested eyes, anemia, coughing, bleeding from the nose and gums, enlarged glands, and abdominal distension.

Prevention: Sorcerers in the Middle East advise people to wear a wreath of walnut leaves, rub themselves with ashes, or take vitamin B_1 tablets daily.

Treatment: This disease is often fatal; therefore, Egyptian shamans, as do others, advise consulting a specialist. In the meantime, they prescribe strict bed rest, oral hygiene, and a well-balanced diet.

Dysentery

Symptoms: Extreme diarrhea, often with the passage of mucus and blood, accompanied by abdominal pains, nausea, and weakness.

Treatment: Russian shamans prescribe a mixture of 1/4 pound of fresh cherries in 1/4 quart of red wine placed in the sun for two days, a wineglass three times daily; for children, a thimbleful.

Hawaiian *kahunas* recommend drinking guava tea several times daily.

Mexican *brujas* feed their patients copious amounts of hot tea with burnt toast, and then blackberry cordial, rice, and cheese.

Ugandan *ngangas* put blackberries, brandy, and raw egg yolks in the patient's porridge. They then sing this incantation, in a secret tongue to the spirits, on a soft-boiled egg nine times for three days: *"Ecce dogola nedit dudum, bethecunda brethecunda, alecunda aleuahge, macte me arenum, ortha, fueba, lata uis leti unda, nosuis terras dulgedob."*

Dysmenorrhea

Symptoms: Periodic pain in women.
Treatment: Folk practitioners in Ireland advise patients to drink gin with horseradish in it, and eat ashberries.

Dyspepsia

Symptoms: Extreme indigestion often due to emotional stress.
Treatment: Hawaiian *kahunas* put their patients on a special diet (see Chapter Four: Diets), while playing Hawaiian music.

Earache

Treatment: Canadian Indian medicine men bake the heart of an onion, place it in the patient's ear, and tie up his head with a woolen scarf.

Ear Trouble

Treatment: For a foreign body in the ear, Greek healers have the patient turn his head to one side; then they gently pour olive oil in the ear so the object will float out.

For wax in the ear, Hungarian gypsies apply a drop of glycerine.

Eczema

An inflammation of the skin.
Symptoms: Red skin with thin yellow crusts.

Treatment: Shamans in Russia apply sulphur and sweet cream to the infected area twice daily.

Electrocution

Treatment: Gypsies in Romania, like other first aiders, advise to shut off the source of power or move the victim with a board before touching him, and when he is free from the wire, apply mouth-to-mouth resuscitation. When he comes to, they feed him a little brandy, and treat him for shock and burns. If a patient has been struck by lightning, they use the same treatment.

Elephantiasis

Symptoms: A disease common in the tropics, and characterized by inflammation of the lymphatic glands. It affects mainly the arms, legs, and scrotum. One leg may become large, like that of an elephant, hence the name "elephantiasis."

Prevention: In Tanzania, natives wear elephant hair bracelets, and attempt to avoid mosquitoes which carry the disease.

Treatment: African *ngangas* in Zimbabwe feed their patients gooseberries, pomegranates, fish, and tea made from the powdered bark of the calotropia plant. If patient does not improve, they may consult with a specialist to prescribe antibiotics.

Emphysema

Symptoms: Difficulty in breathing, coughing, wheezing, swelling of the neck, and sometimes a barrel-like chest.

Treatment: English folk healers advise the patient to quit smoking, and move to a smog-free climate. They apply a comfrey poultice to the swollen neck, and feed him comfrey tea, wheat germ, and mixed green salads.

Enteritis

Inflammation of the bowels.

Primary Symptoms: Fever, fixed pains in the abdomen, costiveness, and vomiting.

Treatment: Chinese herbalists advise no cathartics because they could cause irritation. For the vomiting, they prescribe the leaves of adder's tongue with distilled water of horsetail (shave grass). Then they apply a warm fomentation of stramonium leaves, prepared with equal parts of strong vinegar and water, to the lower abdomen.

Epilepsy

Symptoms: Patient is seized by violent convulsions and fits, from time to time, but does not remember them.

Treatment: In ancient Rome, when a patient had a seizure, healers placed a stick in his mouth so he would not swallow his tongue. Then every night, before bedtime, they placed a pinch of salt on his tongue, and had him drink a little water.

Bavarian gypsies place a wreath of mistletoe around the victim's neck, being careful not to let him eat the poisonous berries.

Erysipelas
(St. Anthony's Fire)

Symptoms: A spreading, inflammatory redness of the skin, with puffy swellings, tenderness, burning, painful tingling, and tension. An attack usually starts with shivering, languor, headache, and vomiting.

Treatment: Shamans in Singapore make a poultice of white navy beans for the skin, and put the patient on a special diet (see Chapter Four: Diets).

In Japan, folk healers apply crushed raw cranberries to the skin.

Eye Trouble

1) Bags under the eyes: Turkish shamans apply wet tea bags.

2) Black eye: Australian folk healers apply raw beef steak to the eye.

3) Blear eye: (An inflammation of the eyelids and corners.) Chinese herbalists bathe the eye with poppy water.

4) Blepharitis: (Inflammation of the lid margins with redness, thickening, and the formation of scales and crusts.) Spanish gypsies have the patient wear golden earrings, and bathe the eye in a solution of baking soda and boiled water.

5) Burns to the eye: Romanian healers apply cold tea to the burn.

6) Cataracts: (A white film over the eye.) In Peru, *curanderos* brew wintergreen leaves in hen's oil, cool, strain, and apply.

Siberian shamans make a hole in a turnip, insert a piece of rock candy, leave overnight in the dew, and apply the liquid to the eye.

Folk healers in Vermont apply a solution of honey and vinegar.

7) Conjunctivitis: (A cold characterized by watering of the eye.) In Nepal, witch doctors dissolve 1/2 teaspoon cayenne pepper in a cup of purified warm water, and bathe the eye several times daily.

8) Foreign bodies in the eye ("speck"): In England, as well as elsewhere, healers hold eyelash out and down over the eyeball until tears wash out the speck, and then they bathe the eye with a weak boric acid solution.

The *nganga* in Uganda applies a poultice of wet sage blossoms.

9) Glaucoma: (Partial blindness in which the patient often sees halos around figures.) Mexican *brujas* feed the

patient fish, shellfish, carrots, lettuce, beets, and beet juice.

10) Iritis: (The colored part of the eye loses its clearness, and a pink zone invades the cornea.) Hungarian gypsies apply a solution of slippery elm bark, or marshmallow root.

11) Myopia: (Nearsightedness.) Russian shamans have the patient exercise the eyes by moving them to the left, then to the right, then up and down several times before sending him to an optometrist for glasses or contact lenses.

12) Pinkeye: (A contagious eye inflammation characterized by redness, soreness, and itching. A mucus discharge seals the lid margins together overnight.) In Turkey, shamans break a raw egg, and apply the last few drops of the egg white, from the shell, into the eye three times daily.

13) Sore eyes: Ugandan *ngangas* apply a piece of raw liver every night to the patient's eye, and have him sleep on it.

14) Sty: (A small boil on the eyelid.) Hungarian gypsies rub the sty with a gold ring.

15) Trachoma: (A serious eye disease common in the Middle East. It is spread by flies, and using a common towel. It is characterized by intense pain and a sensitivity to bright light. A cloudy curtain spreads over the cornea, and small ulcers appear.) Shamans in Iraq bathe the eye with a solution of boric acid and purified water.

In Saudi Arabia, folk healers apply an ointment of lard and cayenne pepper to the afflicted eye.

Abinzas in the Sudan have their patients eat ground cherry pits in peanut butter.

16) Weak eyes: Shamans in Algiers put their patients on a special diet (see Chapter Four: Diets).

17) Xerophthalmia: (Night blindness.) African natives in The Gambia eat oranges, and raw carrots.

Fainting

Treatment: Shamans in Malaysia advise the commonplace approach, placing the patient in a horizontal position with his head lower than his body. They dash cold water in his face, and have him smell spirits of camphor.

Falling of the Womb

Primary Symptons: Bearing down sensations in the womb, dragging and aching pains in the small of the back and around the loins and hips, weariness, soreness, faintness, leukorrheal discharge, nervousness, irritability, and constipation.

Treatment: Bulgarian gypsies put 1/2 ounce of beaver castor in 1/2 pint of gin and give 1 tablespoon three times daily. Then they have the patient take chest-to-knee position on the floor several times daily, while having her avoid housework and exercise.

Fatigue

Treatment: For chronic fatigue, Vermont folk practitioners advise patient to get at least 8 hours of uninterrupted sleep nightly, and have them eat trail mix, chocolate, bee pollen (up to 3 ounces daily), and baked beans sprinkled with vinegar.

Felons

An inflammation of the finger, thumb, or hand.
Symptoms: The pain is very deep with prickling and throbbing.
Treatment: New Zealand Maoris apply a poultice of salt

and the white of an egg, and then rub the felon with a slice of lemon.

Fever

Treatment: Cherokee Indian medicine men prescribe copious amounts of goldenseal tea. Then they sponge the patient's face and body with ice water, and feed him lemon juice in water.

Fever Sores

Treatment: Shamans in Siberia apply fresh scraped turnips to the sores twice daily.

Fingernails, Breaking

Treatment: Mexican *brujas* suggest people soak their fingernails in olive oil, and go on a special diet (see Chapter Four: Diets).

Fistula, Anal

Symptoms: A hard, extremely painful swelling in the anus.

Treatment: In Russia, shamans advise patient to apply petroleum jelly to the fistula, and then sit over a steaming tub of herbs, with a blanket around his shoulders, for 20 minutes, morning and night. The tub usually contains a handful each of bitter herbs, tansy, hops, wormwood, horehound, and catnip. After steaming, he can apply a poultice of powdered linseed and elm bark in a tablespoon of olive oil to the affected part while drinking large amounts of tea made from centaury plants and burdock seed.

Flatulence

Symptoms: A painful, swollen stomach due to excessive gas.

Treatment: The traditional healer in Tahiti promotes burping by having patient eat caraway seeds, and chew vanilla pods.

Flea Bites

Prevention: In Vermont, folk healers take fleabane herb, or moth balls, and sprinkle where fleas inhabit.

Treatment: English healers apply moistened baking soda to bites.

Flies

Prevention: According to Connecticut folk practitioners, flies can be discouraged by hanging a wreath of black walnut leaves in a room.

Fractures

Symptoms: Extreme pain and swelling around a broken bone. Often there is vomiting, especially in the case of skull fractures, and nosebleed in the case of a broken nose.

Treatment: For simple fractures, folk healers in England apply a comfrey poultice, bandage, splint, and call a physician.

In cases of compound fractures, where the skin is broken with the bone protruding, Russian shamans stop the bleeding, apply calendula lotion, bandage, and splint before having it set.

Freckles

Treatment: Scottish healers make a paste of dry mustard and lemon juice, and apply it to the freckles four nights in succession.

Freezing

Symptoms: The patient is usually unconscious and blue.

Treatment: Siberian shamans advise not rubbing the patient with snow, but bundling him in a blanket and thawing him gradually in a warm room while feeding him hot tea with a little brandy.

Witch doctors in Afghanistan have their patients take hot baths, with chopped celery in the water, every night for two weeks.

Eskimos in Greenland apply goose grease, containing polar bear hairs, to the patient's skin, and feed him Beef Tea (see Chapter Five: Health Recipes.)

Frostbite

Destruction of the tissues by freezing.

Symptoms: Blueness, numbness, and swelling.

Treatment: Folk practitioners in Pennsylvania scrape a turnip into a teacup of lard, and stew it slowly on the back of the stove for 24 hours. Then they strain out the turnip, let the lard cool, and apply it to the frostbite every night.

Maoris in New Zealand apply rabbit fat, or a salve made from equal parts of lard and gunpowder, to the affected part.

Fumigation of a Room

In Vermont, folk healers pour vinegar on a hot shovel. To remove foul odors they burn coffee grounds on the stove.

Gallstones

Concretion formed in the gallbladder or bile duct.

Symptoms: The stones are very painful, and are felt to the right of the stomach beneath the lower rib. There is often nausea, anxiety, restlessness, faintness, prostration, and pale skin.

Treatment: Folk healers in Germany have the patient avoid wheat bread, or any foods containing lime. They feed him radishes, and have him drink 6 tablespoons of olive oil, at bedtime, every two days. They also recommend a special diet (see Chapter Four: Diets).

Ganglion

Symptoms: A small, painless swelling formed on one or more tendons on the backs of the wrists.

Treatment: Romanian gypsies bind a piece of lead on the swelling, or paint it with iodine twice daily, and cover it with oiled silk.

Gangrene

Causes: Severe frostbite, injuries, diabetes, or Buerger's disease.

Symptoms: The skin loses feeling and turns black.

Treatment: Mexican *brujas* in Oaxaca apply a cow dung poultice to the afflicted area, and wrap it in newspapers.

The *nganga* in Ghana applies a mashed cooked carrot poultice for ten days.

Russian shamans apply an oatmeal poultice, but if this is ineffective, they call a specialist as the ailment is often fatal.

Gastritis

Inflammation of the stomach.

Symptoms: Pain occurring after eating, morning nausea, gas, extended stomach, weight loss, and often vomiting.

Treatment: Moroccan healers put patients on a special diet (see Chapter Four: Diets), and have them take mustard seeds in water before breakfast.

German Measles
(Rubella)

Primary Symptoms: Mild pink rash on face and body, running nose, mild headache, slight fever, and swelling of the neck glands.

Prevention: Vaccination.

Treatment: Folk healers in Germany warn that this disease is especially dangerous to expectant mothers, and can damage the fetus. They have the patient stay in bed, in a darkened room, and advise drinking sassafras tea twice daily.

Gingivitis

Symptoms: Sore, swollen, or red gums, loose teeth, bad breath, pockets of pus on the gums, often with bleeding; unusual taste in the mouth, and fatigue. If not healed, the patient might need to have his teeth pulled, and be fitted with dentures; otherwise, the poison from the patient's mouth could spread throughout the body, and cause a fatal heart attack.

Treatment: New England folk practitioners suggest brushing teeth after each meal with baking soda and salt dissolved in water, and then rinsing the mouth with 1/3 hydrogen peroxide in 2/3 hot water. They also put the patient on a special diet (see Chapter Four: Diets).

Bomohs in Borneo place a poultice of dead ants on the gums.

Gland Trouble

Symptoms: In some severe cases, redness and soreness develop, which means they are inflammed.

Treatment: Ngangas in Uganda rub the swollen glands lightly with a beryl stone, and chant in a secret tongue: *"Alfa tibi, eddit nota fructu leta."* Then they feed the patient a cup of saw palmetto tea, and put him on a special diet (see Chapter Four: Diets).

Glossitis
(Sore Tongue)

Treatment: Shamans in Greece mix together 2 tablespoons of honey with 1/2 gram of borax. Dose: 1 teaspoon twice daily.

New England folk practitioners advise their patients to drink milk, and eat wheat germ muffins.

Goiter

An enlargement of the thyroid gland often due to the lack of iodine in the diet.

Treatment: Maoris in New Zealand apply the morning's urine, on a cloth, to the swelling daily. They place a string of amber beads around the patient's neck, and feed him seafood, dried kelp, seaweed, iodized salt, white oak bark tea, and bladder wrack tea.

Gonorrhea

A venereal disease characterized by inflammation of the genital mucous membrane of either sex.

Symptoms: Severe scalding and burning pains when passing urine, which is scanty. Later there is a greenish discharge that is often bloody and copious, headache, fever, and restlessness. If not treated, the disease can damage the organs.

Treatment: Hungarian gypsies recommend flaxseed tea with 1/4 ounce of dragon's blood in it, desert tea, watermelon seed tea, and 2 tablespoons of raw potato juice every 2 hours.

Gorings, by Bulls

Treatment: Mexican *brujas* cut off the bull's horn, heat it until it turns black, scrape off the carbon, and apply the carbon to the wound.

Gout

Symptoms: A painful swelling of the big toe, or other joint.

Treatment: Russian shamans advise patients to avoid alcoholic beverages, liver, and sweetbreads. They prescribe

1 raw bud of garlic twice daily, and a glass of cherry juice morning and night.

Kahunas in Hawaii prescribe watercress soup, and a vegetarian diet.

African *ngangas* in Uganda sing this incantation over the patient's painful area seven times: *"Etter sheen etter sock, Et ta leur etta pachk, wipper ai casn easmitter in shi fo leish in shi corne, orn sheip two till and curht mach a mainshore."*

Gray Hair

Prevention: Folk practitioners in Pennsylvania eat cooked potato peelings, and drink Coca Cola.

Treatment: In France, they tint the hair, or make a tea from the root of the grapevine, and wash the hair with it once a month.

In England, after boiling potatoes, they apply the water from the pan to the hair.

Guillain-Barré Syndrome

A disorder of the nervous system causing weakness, and paralysis of the extremities.

Treatment: Quebec folk healers put the patient on a special diet (see Diet for Paralysis in Chapter Four: Diets), and massage his arms and legs often with Vitamin E cream.

Halitosis
(Bad Breath)

Treatment: Folk healers in Italy advise chewing cardamom seeds, and going on a special diet (see Chapter Four: Diets).

Hanging

Treatment: In Bavaria, to revive a person who has been hung, but is still alive, gypsies apply mouth-to-mouth resuscitation, bathe his forehead with vinegar, and pass hartshorn frequently under his nose. When he comes to, they give him a little brandy in a snifter glass.

Hangovers

Prevention: Folk practitioners in France recommend, after heavy alcohol consumption, several glasses of cold water before retiring.

Treatment: Vermont folk healers suggest one of the following:

1) A Bloody Mary (tomato juice with a dash of Worcestershire sauce, a jigger of vodka, and ice.)
2) A Screwdriver (orange juice, a jigger of vodka, and ice.)
3) Celery juice, a dash of soda water, and a drop of Tabasco sauce.
4) A whiff of pure oxygen.
5) A vanilla milk shake.
6) A pineapple ice cream soda.
7) A glass of cold beer.

Hungarian gypsies recommend one of the following remedies:

1) Sauerkraut juice.
2) Raw cabbage dipped in vinegar.
3) Chicken broth with rice.
4) Hot camomile tea with a shot of brandy in it.
5) Lemon juice and baking soda in a half glass of water.

Voodootherapists in New Orleans recommend for the "morning-after": 1/4 each of Pernod and white crème de cacao in 3 ounces of milk, mixed in a blender with cracked ice.

Hay Fever

An allergic disease of mucous membranes of the nose and upper air passages induced by external irritations.

Symptoms: Sneezing, wheezing, and running of the nose and eyes.

Treatment: Canadian Indian medicine men take a pine branch with pine gums and pine needles, boil for three days in water, strain, and thicken with honey, 1 teaspoon four times daily.

Russian shamans prescribe sucking the sap of a fir tree.

Headache

Treatment: Gurus in India put a teaspoon of dried basil in a cup of hot water, cool, and add 2 tablespoons of witch hazel. They dip a compress in the solution, and apply it to the forehead.

Vermont sorcerers wet a brown paper bag with vinegar, sprinkle it generously with black pepper, and apply it to the head.

In Kenya, *ngangas* chant this incantation on a soft-boiled egg nine times: "O pain in thy head, the father of all evil, look upon thee now! Thou has greatly pained thee, thou who tormentest thy head. Remain not in thee! Go thou, go home! Who treads upon thy shadow to him be the pain."

Heart Attacks
(Coronary Thrombosis)

Primary Symptoms: Chest or back pain, extreme radiating pain in the arms, weakness, indigestion, shortness of breath, nausea, and sometimes vomiting.

Prevention: In Bulgaria, gypsies suggest eating sesame seeds to cut down on the cholesterol in the body.

Treatment: Vermont folk practitioners often use conventional cardiopulmonary resuscitation, and call for medical help. They recommend strict bed rest, a special diet (see Chapter Four: Diets), and have the patient avoid tobacco and alcohol.

Ju-ju men in Togo, Africa, wet a cloth with hot water and mustard, and apply it to the heart.

Curanderos in Peru give their patients 1/4 teaspoon cayenne pepper in a cup of water, and sprinkle their food with foxglove.

Mexican *brujas* sprinkle the patient's food with the powdered heart of a bluejay, and have him wear a poinsettia next to his heart.

Chinese herbalists prescribe the powdered head of a toad in wine.

Heartburn

Symptoms: Burning pains around the heart sometimes caused by eating spicy foods.

Treatment: New England folk healers advise drinking 1/2 milk and 1/2 soda water in a tall glass.

Heat Cramps

Symptoms: Extremely painful cramps in the arms, legs, or abdomen due to excessive heat.

Treatment: Persian shamans have the patient lie down in a well-ventilated area with head slightly lower than the body. They feed him 1/2 teaspoon salt in 1/3 glass of water, and have him drink a copious amount of fruit juice.

Heat Prostration

Symptoms: The face is pale, perspiration is profuse, and the entire body is clammy. The pulse is weak, breathing shallow, and weakness extreme. Often there is fainting, nausea, vomiting, and dizziness.

Treatment: Mexican *brujas* have the patient lie down, sponge his head with a wet cloth, and feed him sage tea several times daily.

Heel Spurs

Symptoms: Severe pains in the heel due to a small hard growth; may be caused by wearing ill-fitting shoes.

Treatment: Vermont folk practitioners have the patient wear slippers, and rub the spur with lemon juice.

Hematuria
(Blood in the Urine)

Treatment: Gypsies in Bulgaria prescribe peach leaf tea.

Hemophilia

A hereditary blood disease characterized by the blood refusing to clot.

Treatment: Ngangas in Zimbabwe have their patients drink Liver Tonic Mrewa (see Chapter Five: Health Recipes) twice weekly, and eat foods rich in vitamin K (see Chapter Six: Vitamins and Minerals).

Hungarian gypsies apply pressure to a wound while singing this *icaro:* "In the blood of Adam, sin was taken. In the blood of Christ, it was all shaken. And the same blood I do thee charge. That the blood of (patient's name) run no longer at large."

Hemorrhages

Abnormal internal or external discharge of blood.

Treatment: Shamans in Japan advise applying ice to the source of the bleeding, feeding the patient small amounts of ice, and having him lie down with head and shoulders raised. For stomach hemorrhages, they utilize usual medical care, and feed patient intravenously until recovery.

Folk healers in Siberia feed patients 1/2 teaspoon salt in vinegar and water, alternated with shepherd's purse tea.

Hemorrhoids

Varicose veins of the anus. There are two types: internal and external.

Symptoms: Pain, itching, and bleeding, depending on type.

Treatment: For internal hemorrhoids, Hawaiian *kahunas* prescribe yarrow tea, alternated with Papaya Tea (see Chapter Five: Health Recipes) several times daily.

For external hemorrhoids, Russian shamans prescribe mullein flower tea with honey twice daily. For the pain, they mix 1 tablespoon of raw linseed oil and 3 teaspoons of white lead to make an ointment to be applied twice daily. They recommend the patient go on a special diet (see Chapter Four: Diets), get lots of fresh air and exercise, take a relaxing vacation, sleep on a hard mattress, and take hot sitz baths. For bleeding hemorrhoids, they recommend shepherd's purse, or prince's feather tea twice daily.

Hepatitis

Inflammation of the liver.

Primary Symptoms: Jaundice, loss of appetite, aching of the back, joints, or eyes; heartburn, diarrhea, and nausea.

Prevention: Since the disease is very contagious, many traditional healers advise those who are exposed to be vaccinated. Some also offer the traditional advice against eating shellfish during the months with no "R" in their names.

Treatment: Shamans in Greece prescribe lots of bed rest, a special diet (see Chapter Four: Diets), and dandelion tea.

Hernia

A protrusion or projection of an organ, or a part of an

organ, through the wall of the cavity which normally contains it.

Prevention: Avoid lifting anything too heavy.

Treatment: Brujas in Mexico grind snowberries, add egg whites, a little tequila, and baking soda, place it in a small bag, and apply it to the hernia. They recommend the patient wear a truss, eat lettuce, and drink fruit juices with tequila sunrises.

Herpes Progenitalis

Symptoms: Painful sores on the genital area caused by sexual contact with infected persons, or cross-contamination with one's own, or other people's, cold sores.

Treatment: Hawaiian *kahunas* advise dabbing vinegar on the sores several times daily, and drinking 2 cups of sassafras tea. Then they put the patient on a special diet (see Chapter Four: Diets).

Hiccoughs

Treatment: Hungarian gypsies feed their patients 1 tablespoon of sugar.

The *marabout* in Senegal, as well as other healers, has his patient drink ten sips of water while holding his nose, and then he scares him with a war whoop.

Hives

Treatment: Traditional medicine men in Borneo bind a sack of salt to the back of the patient's neck.

Hoarseness

Treatment: Spanish gypsies advise chewing horseradish root.

Hodgkin's Disease

Symptoms: A malignant swelling of the lymph glands,

accompanied by fever, night sweats, itching, and weight loss.

Treatment: In Haiti, the *houngan* applies a poultice of bruised periwinkle to the swelling, and has the patient sip ice cold champagne. Since the disease is often fatal, if possible, he calls a specialist.

Hornet Stings

Treatment: Witch doctors in New Guinea apply mud to the sting.

Housemaid's Knee

Symptoms: The knee is extremely painful due to the accumulation of water in it.

Prevention: Use a pad when kneeling.

Treatment: Vermont folk practitioners apply dry heat and iodine to the knee, and massage it several times daily. They advise the patient to do no more kneeling until recovered, and go on a special diet (see Chapter Four: Diets).

Hyperactivity

Symptoms: Nervousness and temper tantrums in children. Inability of child to sit quietly and pay attention, accompanied by strange jerking movements.

Treatment: Pennsylvania folk healers advise the patient to drink tea made from powdered valerian root, raspberry leaves, and honey twice daily. Then they put him or her on a special diet (see Chapter Four: Diets).

Hyperventilation

Symptoms: Patient has difficulty breathing because he is exhaling too much carbon dioxide.

Treatment: English folk healers, as well as some medical

doctors, place a paper sack over the patient's head briefly, and have him take short breaths.

Hypoglycemia
(Low Blood Sugar)

Primary Symptoms: Chronic fatigue, headache, buzzing in the ears, and respiratory ailments.

Treatment: Russian shamans advise patients to eat only unprocessed naturally grown foods and nuts, and no sugar or pastries. They have them drink Magic Protein Potion (see Chapter Five: Health Recipes) for breakfast, and vodka and grapefruit juice before dinner.

Hypothermia
(Exposure)

Body temperature below normal due to exposure to cold weather or cold water.

Symptoms: Confusion, bad temper, paleness, and lack of response.

Treatment: Shamans in Lapland advise not allowing the patient to lie down in an unsheltered area, but get him into a warm room as soon as possible. They try to get his temperature up to normal by having him take a hot tub bath, feeding him hot food and hot drinks, and covering him with reindeer fur. If he loses consciousness, they apply artificial respiration.

Hysteria

Symptoms: Depression of spirits, crying, screaming, difficulty in breathing, sickness in the stomach, and a marked craving for sympathy. This ailment is often psychosomatic.

Treatment: The *marabout* in Senegal has the patient drink peppermint tea, and attempts to exorcise the evil spirits form his mind and body. If this is not effective, he might perform a *N'Doep* ceremony.

Impetigo

An inflammatory, contagious skin disease most frequently affecting children.

Symptoms: Pus-filled eruptions on face.

Treatment: Vermont folk practitioners apply apple cider vinegar to the eruptions twice daily.

Impotency

Symptoms: Loss of sexual capability in males.

Treatment: Many potions are suggested for this ailment.

Voodootherapists in New Orleans recommend a special diet (see Diet for Sexual Apathy in Chapter Four: Diets).

African natives in many countries sprinkle the powdered horn of a rhinoceros on their food.

Korean men drink ginseng tea.

In China, powdered sea horse is a popular aphrodisiac.

Japanese folk healers prescribe fish flour in cooking.

Mexican *brujas* in Yucatan make a love potion from the powdered heart of a swallow.

In France, some drink parfait d'amour, and champagne.

In Denmark, absinthe is a favored remedy.

The Haitian *houngan* prescribes 4 ounces rocket seed, 1 ounce honey, and 1 ounce pepper, the whole mixture twice daily.

Indigestion

Treatment: For mild indigestion, English folk healers prescribe peppermint tea, or vodka in a cup of hot bouillon.

In Hawaii, *kahunas* prescribe papaya or Papaya Tea (see Chapter Five: Health Recipes).

Infections

Symptoms: Inflammation, pain, often with pus.

Treatment: Cherokee Indian medicine men place moldy bread (a basis of penicillin) on infected wounds.

Russian shamans prescribe hot poultices of sage applied to the infected area, and have patients drink sage tea several times daily.

Influenza
(The Grippe, Asiatic Flu, London Flu, Swine Flu, or Flu)

Primary Symptoms: Weakness, aches in the joints, high fever, coughing, constipation or diarrhea, and sweating.

Treatment: Folk healers in Israel prescribe strict bed rest, Beef Tea (see Chapter Five: Health Recipes), homemade chicken soup, aspirin, lemon soda, and copious amounts of fruit juice.

Shamans in Guadalcanal prescribe hot tea, with a teaspoon of raspberry jam in it, six or more times daily.

Ingrown Toenail

Symptoms: Inflammation and pain due to the toenail edge growing into the skin.

Treatment: Vermont folk practitioners advise filing a V-groove in the middle of the toenail, and letting it grow upward around the edges.

Hawaiian *kahunas* wrap the affected toe in papaya leaves.

Ngangas in Kenya apply fresh butter to the toe and bandage, brushing it with a cow tail twice daily.

Injuries

Treatment: Hawaiian *kahunas* apply the milky sap from the papaya tree on deep cuts. For infections, they apply a paste made from the roasted seeds of the plantain weed mixed with salt and water.

For an injured finger, the *nganga* in Uganda places the finger in a big hair curler and bandages, while chanting in a secret tongue to the spirits, *"Light, Beff, Cletemati, Donai, Cleona, Florit."*

Insomnia

Treatment: Folk healers in England suggest patients sleep with their heads to the north, and their feet to the south, and drink a cup of hot tea with banana liqueur. They also advise many time-honored "remedies," such as taking a hot bath before bedtime, reading a dull book, and counting sheep.

Intoxication

Symptoms: Slurred speech, inability to walk a straight line, and sometimes falling down.
Prevention: West African *guerisseurs* (healers) advise against drinking heavily on an empty stomach; they recommend eating peanut butter before imbibing alcohol.
Treatment: Folk practitioners in Ireland have the inebriate take a cold shower, and drink copious amounts of black coffee.

Involuntary Urination

Treatment: In Singapore, shamans feed their patients plantain tea four or more times daily.
Vermont folk healers suggest chewing juniper berries.

Jaundice

A disease of the liver.
Symptoms: Yellow eyes and skin, constipation, lassitude, anxiety, pain in the stomach, bitter taste, and fever. It may be caused by the obstruction of bile.
Prevention: Mexican *brujas* recommend eating strawberries.

Treatment: Russian shamans advise that premature babies with jaundice be placed under white fluorescent lights.

Shamans in Egypt suggest that patients drink cold water containing the juice of bruised peach leaves, 1/4 cup four times daily. Later they have them drink flaxseed tea flavored with licorice.

Curanderos in Peru prescribe Peruvian bark in port wine, and put the patient on a special diet (see Chapter Four: Diets).

Jellyfish Stings

Symptoms: Multiple long lines resembling whip marks showing a "ladder pattern." Intense swelling and redness within 5 minutes, and severe pain for from 20 minutes to several hours.

Treatment: Lifeguards in Mexico lay the victim on his back, rub the stings with dry sand, and then apply gin. They sometimes place a tourniquet briefly on the affected limb above the sting, and elevate the limb above the head. If the reaction is severe, they may use other measures and call for medical assistance.

Kidney Stones

Symptoms: Severe pain in the kidney. If the stone is small enough, it may be passed in the urine; however, this is painful.

Prevention: New England folk healers advise those who are susceptible to calcium deposits to avoid dairy products.

Treatment: Hungarian gypsies have patients drink the juice of red onions twice daily, and eat raw asparagus. Then they take a bunch of parsley, stew it in a pint of water, boiled down to 1/2 pint, cool, and add a wineglass full of gin, giving the entire amount every morning.

Kidney Trouble
(Pyelitis)

An infection of the kidneys.

Symptoms: Fever, nausea, pain in the kidneys, loss of appetite, and headache.

Treatment: Natives in the Fiji Islands drink Kava (see Chapter Five: Health Recipes).

Hopi Indian medicine men in Arizona make a tea of cheese weed (malva), and administer it three times daily.

Eskimo healers in Greenland mix cloves, pepper, mustard, and the hairs of a seal in goose grease, and apply it externally to the pain.

Vermont folk practitioners put their patients on a special diet (see Chapter Four: Diets).

Kuru

Symptoms: A rare, usually fatal, laughing disease of New Guinea, brought on by cannibalistic rites.

Treatment: Sorcerers in New Guinea attempt to cure this disease by having the patient drink copious amounts of sage tea daily, and exorcising the evil spirits from his body.

Lameness

Treatment: Folk practitioners in New England take the beaten yolk of an egg, add 1 teaspoon of turpentine, 1 tablespoon of apple cider vinegar, and apply the mixture to the lame part.

Laryngitis

Symptoms: Sore throat and loss of voice.

Treatment: Caribbean calypso singers take 1 part honey, 1 part lime juice, and 4 parts rum to drink.

In France, singers drink white wine with ice.

Mexican *brujas* feed patients bougainvillea flower tea.

Cherokee Indian medicine men prescribe a gargle of vinegar, rain water, and salt several times daily.

Leprosy
(Hansen's Disease)

Symptoms: A skin disease characterized by the degeneration and sloughing off of the flesh. Other symptoms include poor reflexes, and loss of sensation.

Treatment: Gurus in India apply 2 drams of borax, 2 ounces of honey, and 2 ounces of water, morning and night, to the afflicted areas. Then they give the patient 5 drops of chaulmoogra oil daily after lunch, and have him take ultraviolet light treatments.

Brujas in Mexico have their patients eat skunk meat.

Leptospirosis
(Weil's Disease, Canicola Fever, or Fort Bragg Fever)

Symptoms: Patient has an irregular fever with sharp rises and falls, chills, malaise, vomiting, muscular pains (especially of the calf), and congestion of the eyes. A reddish rash may appear, and there may be sore throat, bleeding, enlarged glands, and suppression of urine.

Prevention: Since the disease is usually caused by the excreta of rats, dogs, pigs, and rodents, Mexican *brujas* advise avoiding contaminated water.

Treatment: Irish folk healers feed the patient 2 tablespoons of raw potato juice every 4 hours, have him stay in bed, and put him on a diet of milk and bland food even after temperature has subsided.

Turkish shamans apply soft-boiled eggs, cooked in sweet butter, to the patient's eyes, and rub his calves with eel oil.

Leukemia

Symptoms: A form of blood cancer in which the white cells multiply, and the red cells diminish. It is usually a painless, but often fatal, disease, and is characterized by anemia.

Treatment: Shamans in Czechoslovakia have the patient eat oranges, mixed green salads, and raw vegetables while wearing an "Infant of Prague" medal around his neck. If possible, they call a cancer specialist.

Leukorrhea

A common female disorder characterized by a whitish vaginal discharge. During ovulation, it might be tinged with blood.

Treatment: Russian shamans prescribe the juice of fresh barberries, one small wineglass per day. If the discharge becomes more profuse or changes color, to yellowish or greenish discharge, they might call a cancer specialist.

Yugoslavian gypsies recommend oregano in dew mixed with peach pits in brandy, administering 1 teaspoon tree or four times daily.

Lice

Lice are very small, but may be seen if one looks closely.

Symptoms: Extreme itching.

Treatment: African *ngangas* in Zimbabwe mix larkspur seed and boiling water, cool, and apply daily. Then every other day they apply hot vinegar to the skin.

Locomotor Ataxia
(Tabes Dorsalis)

A disease of the nervous system sometimes due to an advanced case of syphilis.

Primary Symptoms: Absence of reflexes, incoordination, staggering gait, inability to touch the nose with the finger, "lightning" pains in the legs, and later cystitis, impotence, and trophic ulcers.

Treatment: In Mexico *brujas* recommend massage, exercise, and bathing at local spas. They advise the patient to eat well-balanced meals with spinach and rose hips tea.

Longevity

Natives in India eat gotu kola, to foster longevity.

In China, many people drink fo-ti-tieng tea, and chrysanthemum wine.

In Korea, ginseng tea is popular.

Loose Teeth

Treatment: Healers in Israel make a mouthwash of powdered myrrh and water, having the patient rinse his mouth with it twice daily, after brushing his teeth with baking soda.

Lumbago

Symptoms: Rheumatism involving the lumbar muscles, on one or both sides of the loins.

Treatment: Shamans in Barbados have the patient wear a skein of silk around his waist, and carry a nutmeg in his pocket. He then has the patient exercise the affected part, rubs it with a liniment of olive oil and eucalyptus leaves, and feeds the patient 1 teaspoon of black cohosh tea every 4 hours.

Lung Diseases

Treatment: In Russia, shamans suggest giving the patient a whiff of pure oxygen every 4 hours, or as needed.

The *nganga* in Uganda chants this incantation five times daily to all lung patients: *"Catari Duni Chini Brini."*

Malaria

A tropical disease caused by the bite of an infected mosquito; most common in low coastal areas.

Symptoms: Severe shivering, high fever, profuse sweating, delirium, and stomach cramps. Once the patient contracts this disease, it will recur from time to time.

Treatment: Curanderos along the Amazon River prescribe the bodies of daddy longleg spiders to be added to the patient's gruel, and a tonic made from rose leaves, lemon juice, and Peruvian bark in wine.

Folk healers in Guadalcanal advise complete bed rest, and a special diet (see Chapter Four: Diets) until recovered. If possible, they call a specialist as the disease can be fatal.

Russian shamans prescribe lilac tea several times daily.

Marasmus

Emaciation and wasting away due to poor assimilation of food; more common to infants.

Treatment: Ngangas in Zimbabwe draw a circle around the patient's bed with chalk, and place these good luck charms within the circle: a piece of garlic, an amber bead, some black glass (or obsidian), and a piece of red yarn, while dancing around the room.

In Hawaii, *kahunas* feed patients milk, cream, coconut cream, Rice Water, Barley Water (see Chapter Five: Health Recipes), and later orange juice.

New England folk practitioners put their patients on a special diet for assimilation (see Chapter Four: Diets).

Mastoiditis

Inflammation of the middle ear.

Symptoms: Pain over the mastoid bone and occasional swelling behind the auricle; profuse discharge in the external canal is likely.

Treatment: Turkish shamans blow tobacco smoke in the patient's ear.

Measles

Symptoms: A sore throat, with a raspberry rash on face and body which turns purple; languor and fever. Once the patient has had this disease, he is generally immune for life.

Treatment: Vermont folk practitioners keep the patient in a dark room, feed him flaxseed tea and sassafras tea, along with a bland diet of boiled rice, fruits, berries, and white bread. They sponge the rash often with apple cider vinegar.

Melancholia

A mental disorder characterized by marked depression, physical and mental apathy, brooding, mournful, and doleful notions, and inhibition of activity.

Treatment: The *nganga* in Uganda dresses himself in emu feathers, and dances around the patient three times, chanting: *"Kati kua nui tena."* He then applies his cupping horn to the patient's stomach and "sucks out" the evil spirits.

Gurus in India have patients wear lapis lazuli amulets, and try to keep them so busy they have no time to brood.

Meniere's Disease

An acute disturbance of the inner ear called the labyrinth.

Symptoms: Deafness, ringing in the ears, dizziness, vomiting, and sudden movements of the eyes from side to side.

Treatment: Shamans in Afghanistan put the patient on a high-protein, low-salt diet (see Chapter Four: Diets), and place black wool in his ears.

Meningitis

Inflammation of the meninges of the brain and spinal cord. This disease is highly contagious, and often fatal.

Primary Symptoms: Sore throat, fever, chills, rapid pulse, confusion, irritability, headache, stiff back, general soreness of the body, drowsiness, stupor, and sometimes coma.

Treatment: Ugandan *ngangas* have the patient wear an amulet containing mugwort, and chant this incantation in a secret tongue to the spirits: *"Tolam te artemsia, ne lassus sim in via."*

Hawaiian *kahunas* wrap the patient in a blanket, soak his feet in hot water with mustard, and feed him ginger tea. If possible, they move him to a private room in a hospital.

Bulgarian gypsies rub the patient's back with red pepper and brandy, and feed him 1 tablespoon of raw potato juice every 2 hours. Then they put him on a special diet (see Chapter Four: Diets), while having him maintain absolute bed rest in an isolated, well-ventilated area.

Menopause

Symptoms: Depression, general ability, and hot flashes may accompany menopause.

Treatment: Chinese herbalists prescribe licorice, and vitamin E.

Menorrhagia

Symptoms: Profuse monthly bleeding in women.

Treatment: Russian shamans prescribe iced prince's feather tea.

Mental Disorder
(Dementia)

Causes: A disorder of the mind caused by brain damage, such as a blow to the head, cerebral tumor, alcoholism, meningitis, encephalitis, or senility. Other types of dementia may be hereditary: mental retardation, Down's syndrome, and Huntington's disease. Other forms are manifested in Alzheimer's or Pick's disease, or caused by severe emotional stress.

Ancient Romans attributed some types of mental illness to the effects of the full moon—hence, the word "lunatic."

Primary Symptoms: Memory loss, abrupt personality change, a split personality (schizophrenia), phobias of guilt and persecution (paranoia), depression, a morbid fear of germs (or the other extreme: slovenliness and uncleanliness), hysteria, delusions of grandeur, a desire to commit suicide, and sometimes a desire to injure or kill others.

Treatment: In West Africa, traditional healers have established therapeutic villages where mental patients can reside with one or two members of their families. The therapeutic villages are built to resemble ordinary villages as the traditional healer believes that patients are more apt to recover in cheerful, familiar surroundings. They encourage him to engage in social activities: parties, dances, and tea drinking, in order to return to a world of reality. Often, psychiatrists work together with *marabouts* employing group therapy where patients can discuss and help solve their problems.

African witch doctors reputedly have great success in treating mental patients by "magical means." Ju-ju men on the Ivory Coast help mental patients by exorcising the evil spirits from their minds and bodies, usually by shaking rattles, and having them drink honey and salt from a seashell before sunrise.

Ngangas in Uganda make an amulet for the patient to wear around his neck, consisting of the stinger of a scorpion, the extremity of the basil herb, and a swallow's heart, all in a deer's skin.

For schizophrenia, South African *sangomas* put their

patients on a special diet (see Chapter Four: Diets), and have them get a maximum of sun and outdoor exercise.

Mercurial Disease

Primary Symptoms: Soreness of gums and mouth, looseness of teeth, constant and profuse saliva.

Treatment: Canadian Indian medicine men have the patient drink sage tea with honey. Then they place an amulet around his neck, on a red string, containing an elk's tooth, a piece of red wool, and a walnut.

Metritis

Inflammation of the womb.

Primary Symptoms: Chills, great thirst, nausea, vomiting, diarrhea, and throbbing pains in the womb, which is swollen. Often the tongue is "dirty yellow" coated.

Treatment: Folk healers in the Balkans feed patients spearmint tea, and a tea made from marshmallow roots, pumpkin seeds, or flaxseed.

Migraine Headache

Symptoms: Severe chronic headaches, often on just one side of the head.

Treatment: South African *sangomas* recommend a special diet (see Chapter Four: Diets), and a relaxing vacation.

Bavarian gypsies suggest the patient take a hot bath while blowing bubbles in a pan of ice water.

Romanian shamans recommend visiting a spa for mineral baths, and sitting under a hair dryer while drinking willow bark tea.

Miliaria
(Heat Rash or Prickly Heat)

Causes: Profuse perspiration in hot humid climates.

Symptoms: A pink rash characterized by burning and itching.

Treatment: Witch doctors in Samoa advise patients to take cold showers with no soap, and dust the skin with cornstarch.

Mexican *brujas* put the patient on a low-salt diet (see Chapter Four: Diets). Then, while playing a tambourine and singing, they put a few drops of eucalyptus oil in the rubbing alcohol, and splash it on the rash, after which they put him in an air-conditioned room, and feed him oranges and tomatoes.

Milk Leg

Primary Symptoms: Sometimes this ailment occurs shortly after childbirth. The attack is preceded by a chill, and succeeded by a fever. The leg becomes stiff, heavy, and tender. It is not discolored, but has an increase in heat. After about two weeks these symptoms subside, but the leg may still be stiff and weak.

Treatment: Vermont folk healers bathe the whole limb in a strong solution of salt and vinegar. They put the patient to bed, with the affected leg elevated on a pillow, and never let her put it on the floor until recovery is complete. Since the condition can be fatal, they usually call a medical specialist.

Cherokee Indian medicine men bruise fresh stramonium leaves, moisten with hot water, and apply it to the whole leg.

An ancient Egyptian remedy was to give the patient the tincture of aconite root and since it is poisonous, only 5 drops in a glass of water, 1 teaspoon every 4 hours, under supervision of the healer.

Miscarriage

Symptoms: Pains in the lower abdomen in pregnant women, followed by bleeding and leading to abortion.

Treatment: Irish folk healers have the patient lie down, give her a whiskey highball to drink slowly, and apply cold cloths to the lower abdomen. They have her remain in bed until all danger has passed, and then avoid lifting anything heavy.

In Yugoslavia, gypsies have the patient stay in bed for ten days, and feed her a well-balanced diet with red raspberry leaf tea. If miscarriage occurs, they have her drink camomile tea in which a gold ring has been boiled.

Moles
(and Liver Spots)

Symptoms: Large brown spots on the skin.

Treatment: Russian shamans apply castor oil nightly, claiming this will make the mole, or liver spots, disappear in about four weeks.

Mononucleosis

Prevention: Italian shamans have teen-agers wear strings of garlic around their necks.

Kahunas in Hawaii prescribe asafetida leis.

Causes: This disease frequently occurs in young adults, and is spread by kissing, or other close contact.

Primary Symptoms: Sore throat, swollen lymph glands, extreme weakness, and fever.

Treatment: Vermont folk healers prescribe complete bed rest, and sassafras tea twice daily, along with a nourishing diet.

Morning Sickness

Symptoms: Nausea and vomiting, in the mornings, during the first few months of pregnancy.

Treatment: An ancient Roman remedy was to have the patient drink lime juice and cinnamon in water every morning while afflicted.

Hawaiian *kahunas* prescribe ginger tea.

Mosquito Bites

Prevention: West African ju-ju men hang a wreath of sweet clover in a room.

Hawaiian *kahunas* recommend leis of pennyroyal leaves.

Treatment: Mexican *brujas* apply baking soda in cold cream to bites.

Multiple Sclerosis

A chronic, slowly progressive disease of the central nervous system. According to the Multiple Sclerosis Society, this disease is more prevelant in cold harsh climates with high standards of domestic hygiene.

Primary Symptoms: Muscular weakness, tremor, and paralysis often of the eyes or legs, affecting mainly young adults.

Treatment: Canadian Indian medicine men prescribe blueberries, organically grown raw foods, and a maximum of sun and exercise, while having patient avoid dairy products and animal fats in the diet.

Mumps

Symptoms: Swollen cheeks, headache, and slight fever. Rare complications can cause sterility in boys.

Treatment: Balkan folk practitioners apply mashed string beans to the swellings and any sore spots on the body. Then they have the patient drink large amounts of sage tea, while avoiding all meat and dairy products in the diet.

Muscular Cramps

Treatment: In ancient Egypt, shamans fed the patient 2 teaspoons of honey at each meal.

Muscular Dystrophy

Atrophy and wasting of the muscles; most common in

children. If it progresses, the patient may become crippled.

Primary Symptoms: A waddling gait, frequent falls, difficulty in rising, toe-walking, and a flat smile.

Treatment: Folk healers in Bulgaria massage the patient's limbs with a liniment of vinegar and cayenne pepper. Then they send him to a spa for sunbathing and swimming in mineral waters, while prescribing a special diet (see Chapter Four: Diets).

Myasthenia Gravis

A chronic, often fatal, disease of the nervous system.

Primary Symptoms: Abnormal fatigability and weakness of the muscles, especially of the face and neck. Often the patient is so weak and exhausted he is unable to hold anything in his hands, keep his eyes open, or feed himself.

Treatment: Shamans in Korea prescribe ginseng tea several times daily.

Curanderos in Argentina recommend maté tea, and beet juice, along with a well-balanced diet. If the patient does not improve, they call a medical specialist.

Myelitis

Inflammation of the spinal cord.

Primary Symptoms: Headache on one side of the head, nausea, nightmares, sleeplessness, cold hands and feet, alternate chills and flushes, and pains in the spine.

Treatment: Mexican *brujas* place the patient in a straight chair, have him sit erect, and massage his spine daily with salt water.

Gurus in India suggest patients take yoga exercises.

Narcotic Addiction

Symptoms: The withdrawal symptoms of narcotics, especially heroin, are very severe, and include extreme nervousness, stomach cramps, trembling, and profuse perspiration.

Treatment: Turkish shamans have their patients take diminishing doses of the drug until they are free of their addiction.

Persian witch doctors prescribe that patients drink fermented camel's milk rather than taking drugs.

Mexican *brujas* advise outdoor exercise, and well-balanced meals. In the case of an overdose of narcotics, they feed the patient copious amounts of strong black coffee, and have him walk in the fresh air.

Gurus in India have their patients chew Indian snakeroot.

Nephritis

An inflammatory disease of the kidneys.

Symptoms: Fever, headache, nausea, vomiting, and edema.

Treatment: Curanderos in Peru put their patients on a low-salt diet (see Chapter Four: Diets), and have them drink Coca Cola syrup in plain water, fruit juice, and clove tea.

Nervous Tension

Symptoms: Extreme irritability and sensitivity to noise.

Treatment: Houngans in Haiti recommend hot baths, with a few drops of pine oil added, while burning dragon's blood incense.

In India, gurus have their patients drink passion flower tea, and chew Indian snakeroot.

Russian shamans recommend hot baths in dried lavender flowers.

Ju-ju men in West Africa put their patients on a special diet (see Chapter Four: Diets), and have them eat raw celery.

Hawaiians believe in *hoo ponopono* ("setting things

right")—then they can laugh, dance, and have a good time.

Nettle Rash

Symptoms: Hives, which are roundish or oblong, pale in the center, and red at the circumference, attended by smarting and itching.

Treatment: New England folk practitioners bathe the hives with vinegar, and then rub them with buckwheat flour. They put the patient on a special diet (see Chapter Four: Diets), and have him drink sassafras tea twice daily.

Neuralgia

Symptoms: Severe stabbing, or shooting, pains in the head, often brought on by drafts.

Treatment: Hungarian gypsies soak a piece of cotton cloth in the white of an egg, apply large quantities of black pepper, and apply it to the painful area.

Neurasthenia

This disease may result from a thiamine deficiency, leading to beriberi.

Symptoms: Fatigue, sinus disturbances, irritability, poor memory, gas pains, constipation, and emotional instability.

Treatment: Tahitian folk healers put their patients on a special diet (see Chapter Four: Diets), and have them chew vanilla pods.

Neuritis

An inflammation of certain nerves.

Primary Symptoms: Tingling "pins-and-needles," burning, boring, stabbing pains, and tender nerve trunks.

Treatment: Folk healers in Israel have their patients eat potato soup.

Nightmares

Ju-ju men in Togo have the patient drink thyme tea. Then they place an amulet of garnets around his neck, cross his socks, put a silver pin on them, and hang them on the foot of his bed.

Night Sweats

Symptoms: Heavy perspiration while sleeping.
Treatment: Healers in Vermont bathe patients with vinegar.

Nosebleed

Treatment: Ngangas in Uganda place a piece of folded paper between the patient's gum and upper lip, tie a red string around his little finger, and have him remain quiet.

Navajo Indian medicine men press a wet key to the back of the patient's neck.

Nymphomania

Symptoms: Excessive sexual desire in females.
Treatment: Turkish shamans make a tincture of the root of the yellow pond lily; they bruise the root, put it in a bottle of gin, and let it stand for ten days, shaking it a little each day, giving the patient 10 drops three times daily, under their supervision.

Ophthalmia

Symptoms: Blurred vision, neuralgic pain, and eyeball tenderness, often due to an injured eye.
Treatment: Chinese herbalists make a lotion of quince seeds in distilled water, and apply to the eye. Then they apply a poultice of bruised eyebright herb.

Orchitis

Inflammation of the testicles.

Primary Symptoms: Pain, swelling, chills, fever, and vomiting.

Treatment: Yugoslavian gypsies apply bruised comfrey leaves to the painful area, and have the patient eat pumpkin seeds, and drink comfrey tea several times daily.

Osteomyelitis

An infection of the bones.

Primary Symptoms: Pain, fever, and swelling and redness of the infected area.

Treatment: Polish shamans apply bruised comfrey leaves in hot water to the painful area, and feed the patient 1 tablespoon of raw potato juice every 4 hours.

Osteoporosis

Symptoms: This disease is characterized by weak, brittle bones, and sometimes a "dowager's hump" on the back.

Treatment: Ngangas, in Uganda, sprinkle their patients' porridge with bonemeal, and put them on a special diet (see Chapter Four: Diets).

Otitis

Inflammation of the ear, often associated with swimming.

Symptoms: Pain, and running of the ear.

Treatment: Russian shamans put 10 grains of boric acid in 1 ounce of vodka, and drop 3 drops of the solution into the ear three times daily.

Otomycosis

A fungus infection of the external ear.

Symptoms: Itching, pain, and stinging in the ear.

Treatment: Folk practitioners in New England dilute

aluminum acetate solution in vinegar, and apply it to the ear.

Ovarian Cysts

Primary Symptoms: Severe pain in the lower abdomen, often accompanied by swelling.

Treatment: Hungarian gypsies combine 2 ounces of licorice root with 1 ounce each of comfrey, yarrow, yellow dock, and dandelion root, boiled for 1 hour in a pint of water and strained, and give 1 tablespoon three times daily. They may also call a medical specialist.

Ozena
(Atrophic Rhinitis)

A disease affecting the mucous membrane of the nose.

Symptoms: Large, foul-smelling crusts form on the nose.

Treatment: Hawaiian *kahunas* dissolve cane sugar in water, and spray the patient's nose with it from an atomizer.

Mexican *brujas* advise patients to eat well-balanced meals which include meat, fish, egg yolks, vegetables, milk, cereals, and dark bread.

Pain

Treatment: In ancient Egypt, healers practiced "magnetism" to relieve pain. The sorcerer held his hand over the painful area for a few minutes, passing his fingers over it lightly from right to left, and then passing his hand along the arm or leg to the extremities, making the pain disappear in the air.

In New Guinea, the witch doctor spits on the painful area, and then applies an ointment of mugwort, hog's grease, and field daisies.

In Oaxaca, the Mexican *bruja* takes thirteen seeds of the *ololiuqui* plant, soaks them in water, and has the patient chew them. She then has him spit the seeds out. She pounds the residue into a salve, and applies them to the painful area while singing this *icaro* in Spanish: "Come hither, thou come and expel the green pain, the brown pain, which now wishes to take away the life of the son of the Gods."

Kahunas in Hawaii play soothing Hawaiian music on ukeleles for their patients, and keep chanting: "The pain is going away."

Russian shamans take a hot hard-boiled egg, peel it, cut it in two, and apply the halves to the painful area. As the egg cools, the pain is supposed to disappear.

Navajo Indian medicine men sometimes suggest that their patients chew peyote, an herb which produces hallucinations.

Painter's Colic

Colic accompanying lead poisoning; therefore, painters should always paint in a well-ventilated room, and use water base, rather than lead base paints, when possible.

Primary Symptoms: Vomiting and pain, sometimes leading to palsy and paralysis.

Treatment: Hungarian gypsies prescribe spearmint tea.

Palsy
(Paralysis Agitans)

Symptoms: Giddiness, drowsiness, numbness, dimness of sight, forgetfulness, eye and mouth drawn to one side, incoherent speech, and paralysis of the mouth, eyes, fingers, hands, or arm.

Treatment: In India, gurus take 1 ounce of Indian hemp root, steep for 1 hour in 1 pint of water, and give the patient 2 tablespoons three times daily.

Paralysis

A condition affecting the nervous system characterized by the loss of motion and feeling in certain parts of the body. Hemiplegia is the paralysis of one entire side of the body, and paraplegia is the paralysis of the lower half of the body.

Treatment: Haitian *houngans* put the patient on a special diet (see Chapter Four: Diets), and massage the affected parts with alcohol.

Brujas in Mexico take common oats, pound it in a mortar, put a coffee cupful in a pint of gin with 1/2 pint of water, let it stand for fourteen days, and feed the patient 1 teaspoon three times daily. They also recommend mineral baths at local spas.

Paratyphoid Fever

Causes: Contact with infected animals, infected poultry, or contaminated water.

Prevention: Vaccination is good for three years.

Primary Symptoms: Diarrhea, high fever, and headache.

Treatment: In the Sudan, shamans put 2 tablespoons tincture of wild indigo in 3 tablespoons of water, 1 teaspoon every 2 hours.

Parkinson's Disease

Primary Symptoms: A disease of the central nervous system characterized by incoordination, tremor and stiffening of the muscles, and difficulty in walking and talking.

Treatment: Shamans in Russia advise their patients to eat beets with cooked beet tops two or three times weekly, and go on a special diet (see Chapter Four: Diets). If possible, they consult a medical specialist.

Parrot Fever
(Ornithosis or Psittacosis)

Causes: Contact with, or eating, diseased birds, especially parrots, parakeets, or pigeons.

Primary Symptoms: Fever, chills, headache, backache, malaise, and dry coughing.

Treatment: Curanderos in Peru feed their patients lime-ade, and Shaman Surprise (see Chapter Five: Health Recipes), and have them rest in bed for at least two weeks. If possible, they call a medical specialist as the disease is often fatal.

Parry's Disease
(Hyperthyroidism or Graves' Disease)

Primary Symptoms: Nervousness, weakness, sensitivity to heat, weight loss with increased appetite, restlessness, nausea, sweating, headache, abdominal pain, swollen glands, and diarrhea.

Treatment: Shamans in Iceland have patients drink speedwell tea six times daily, eat seaweed, kelp, seafood, and iodized salt.

Pellagra

Causes: The deficiency of niacin in the body.

Primary Symptoms: Diarrhea, dermatitis, and mental impairment.

Treatment: Voodootherapists in Haiti burn pink candles, and put their patients on a special diet (see Chapter Four: Diets).

Pericarditis

An inflammation of the pericardium which covers and encloses the heart.

Primary Symptoms: Pain over the heart, a rise in pulse rate and temperature, and coughing.

Treatment: Shamans in Italy feed the patient one raw bud of garlic daily, and put him on a low-salt diet (see Chapter Four: Diets).

Chinese herbalists place a hot towel on the patient's heart, and feed him the powdered head of a toad (a source of digitalis) in white wine.

Cherokee Indian medicine men sprinkle foxglove (a small amount, because it is a poisonous herb) in the patient's porridge.

Hawaiian *kahunas* have their patients drink watercress juice, 2 tablespoons three or four times daily.

Peritonitis

An inflammation of the lining membrane of the abdomen.

Causes: An abdominal injury, or complications from appendicitis.

Primary Symptoms: Chills, full, strong and frequent pulse, red eyes, flushed face, short, quick breathing, dry tongue with red edges, dry skin, restlessness, nausea, and tenderness around the abdomen.

Treatment: Israeli healers place the patient on his back with feet drawn up, put hot towels on his abdomen, and put him on a special diet (see Chapter Four: Diets). Since the disease is often fatal, they usually call a medical specialist.

Medicine men in Egypt give patients tincture of aconite root (only 10 drops in 10 tablespoons of water, as the herb is generally poisonous). Supervising the treatment, they administer 1 tablespoon of this diluted mixture every hour until symptoms abate, then 1 tablespoon every 4 hours.

Phlebitis

Inflammation of the veins.

Causes: Blood clots in the blood vessels.

Symptoms: Pain in the veins, fever, chills, and sometimes swelling.

Treatment: Russian shamans advise patients to sleep with their legs elevated, and wear a semi-elastic bandage for ten days.

New Zealand Maoris feed their patients oatmeal water, royal jelly (from queen bees), and raw onions for breakfast.

Pica

This is a condition of general debility affecting children and young people who eat a special kind of white clay in the southern part of the United States.

Symptoms: Pale greenish skin, loss of appetite, and a craving for chalk, coal, cinders, or clay. The patient is often listless and melancholy, and has bad breath.

Treatment: Folk healers in New Orleans put the patient on a well-balanced diet of milk, fish, meat, brown bread, and vegetables, and have him get a maximum of sun and exercise, especially swimming in the sea.

Pilonidal Cyst

This is a cyst containing hair, found at the base of the spine.

Symptoms: Sometimes the cyst becomes inflamed, swollen and painful, developing into a draining fistula excreting pus.

Treatment: Brujas in Peru have patients take hot sitz baths.

Pinworms

Symptoms: Loss of weight, and vomiting up small worms.

Treatment: In Bulgaria, gypsies feed the patient no food except raw apples for three days, with a little water or coffee. On the evening of the third day they feed him 1/2 cup of olive oil.

Spanish gypsies feed patients pumpkin seeds.

Pityriasis Rosea

A skin disease with lesions characterized by the presence of bran-like scales of skin.

Symptoms: It may start with a red spot on the chest, and spread to cover the chest, abdomen, legs, and thighs.

Treatment: Shamans in Romania advise sunbathing and exposure to ultraviolet light during the first two weeks. This usually alleviates the condition, but if not, it may last for three months.

Plethora

A morbid condition believed in some cultures to be characterized by an excess of blood in the system.

Symptoms: The patient feels bloated.

Treatment: In Europe, during the Dark Ages, folk healers bled their patients, often with leeches.

Italian shamans feed their patients a bud of raw garlic.

Cherokee Indian medicine men put their patients on a special diet (see Chapter Four: Diets), and have them drink sassafras tea.

Pleurisy

An inflammation of the pleura, a membrane which lines the inside of the chest. Sometimes it is caused by having perspiration obstructed, such as drinking cold liquids when the body is hot.

Symptoms: Chills, followed by heat and thirst. There is a sharp pain on one side which gradually extends to the shoulder blade. Sometimes the patient coughs up blood.

Treatment: Witch doctors in Borneo apply hot oatmeal poultices to the painful parts, and have the patient drink pleurisy root tea six or more times daily, while keeping quiet in a bolstered position. Then they apply a sack of browned salt under his shoulder blades, and feed him gruel, frequent sips of cold water, and Arrowroot Water (see Chapter Five: Health Recipes)—nothing else until he is recovered. If possible, they consult a medical specialist as the disease is often fatal.

Pneumonia

An acute inflammation of the lung, often caused by complications of colds, bronchitis, influenza, or exposure.

Primary Symptoms: Headache, fever, chest pains, pain in the back and legs, painful breathing, and coughing.

Treatment: Sangomas in South Africa recommend a light diet containing Beef Tea, Barley Water (see Chapter Five: Health Recipes), and skimmed milk. Later they add Shaman Surprise (see Chapter Five: Health Recipes), and homemade chicken soup. Since the disease is often fatal, they may consult with a Western doctor about administering oxygen, antibiotics, or other treatments.

The *nganga* in Uganda finds a lemon tree, beats it, gathers the leaves that fall to earth with the upper surfaces remaining up, boils them in water, and has the patient inhale the steam. Then he has him drink lemonade, containing 1 teaspoon cream of tartar, several times daily.

In Tibet, shamans apply a Mustard Plaster (see Chapter Five: Health Recipes) or a heated oats poultice to the chest, and have the patient drink yak butter tea two or three times a day.

Poison Oak
(and Poison Ivy)

Symptoms: A burning, itching rash extending over the body.

Prevention: Hungarian gypsies advise not touching poison oak, or poison ivy, but instead kill the plants by spraying them with a solution of 1 gallon of soapy water and 3 pounds of salt.

Treatment: Canadian Indian medicine men advise washing thoroughly with yellow kitchen soap after coming in contact with poison oak or poison ivy. If a rash breaks out, they boil string beans, mash, and apply to the skin.

Poisons and Their Antidotes

Symptoms: Pains and burning sensations in the stomach, an intolerable thirst, sweating, convulsion, and delirium. Death often occurs rapidly.

Treatment: Russian shamans advise discovering the poisoning agent by reading the labels on the suspect bottles. They recommend the following antidotes which are readily available to them:

Acid poisoning: They do not give the patient any water, but feed him soapsuds in milk. After the acid is neutralized, they feed him flaxseed tea, gruel, large quantities of milk, and Barley Water (see Chapter Five: Health Recipes), while having him smell ammonia.

Aconite poisoning: They feed the patient mustard in warm water.

Alkali poisoning (such as ammonia or lye): They give the patient vinegar by the teaspoonful, and then olive oil.

Creosote poisoning (such as foxglove or oleander): Large doses of mustard and warm water to promote vomiting, and then large quantities of milk.

Iodine and iodide of potassium: Flour mixed in water.

Lunar caustic poisoning, or nitrate or silver poisoning (found in hair dyes and ink): A strong solution of salt and water; followed by milk, and castor oil.

Narcotic poisoning (such as belladonna, stramonium, opium, or morphine): Strong black coffee, followed by mustard, or grease, in warm water.

Phosphorous poisoning (matches): Mustard in warm water to promote vomiting; then milk of magnesia, followed by flaxseed tea. They have the patient avoid oils and oily drinks.

Rat and insect poisoning (such as arsenic and strychnine): To promote vomiting, they give mustard, warm milk or warm water, mixed with oil, butter, or lard, or feed the patient raw egg whites.

Poliomyelitis
(Infantile Paralysis)

Primary Symptoms: A stiff neck, sudden paralysis of one or more limbs, fever, vomiting, convulsions, and sometimes coma.

Prevention: The Sabin vaccine orally.

Treatment: The witch doctor in Zimbabwe has the patient take a hot bath, massages his paralyzed parts, and feeds him 2/3 hot port wine and 1/3 cinnamon. He then rolls his *hakatas* (special dice) to see if, and when, the patient will recover. Sometimes he burns pink candles, and presents the patient with a coral amulet.

Hawaiian *kahunas* put taro poultices on the paralyzed limbs, and put the patient on a special diet (see Diet for Paralysis in Chapter Four: Diets). They also consult a medical specialist as the disease is often fatal.

Polycythemia

An increase in the red blood cells over the normal amount. This may be temporary due to living in a high altitude, or to breathing too much carbon monoxide.

Symptoms: Dizziness, fainting, ringing in the ears, nosebleed, a feeling of fullness in the head, headache, and a bluish cast to the skin.

Treatment: Shamans in Italy prescribe one raw bud of garlic daily.

Ngangas in Uganda bleed the patient with a cupping horn.

Polyps

A growth of body tissue with a smooth surface and a strange shape; occurring most frequently on the nose.

Treatment: Gurus in India have the patient snuff 2 teaspoons of powdered bloodroot up the afflicted nostril, a little at a time.

Post Nasal Drip

Symptoms: Sore throat and bad breath; usually caused by a cold, with mucus from the nose discharging into the throat.

Treatment: Mexican *brujas* advise patients to stop smoking, or cut down, and move to a dry climate.

New Zealand Maoris sprinkle paprika on the patient's food, have him eat bananas, and drink grape juice rather than orange juice.

Pregnancy

Primary Symptoms: Absence of the menses, a craving for unusual foods, morning sickness, dizziness, faintness, poor circulation in the feet, swollen and tender breasts, fatigue, limp hair, and later a swollen stomach.

Treatment: Vermont folk practitioners prescribe a well-balanced, low-salt diet (see Chapter Four: Diets), and advise the patient not to gain more than 20 pounds in nine months.

Hungarian gypsies have the patient drink copious amounts of red raspberry leaf tea for a less painful childbirth. (They put a ring on a string—preferably a wedding ring, and hold it over the expectant mother's stomach. If it swings around in a circle, the baby will be a girl, and if it swings back and forth, a boy.)

Prevention of Disease

Vermont folk practitioners, and other healers, advise those traveling to foreign countries not to drink the water, or milk, unless it is purified. Alcoholic beverages, they believe, may be consumed in moderation to "kill germs," but the best prevention of disease is to eat well-balanced meals, with eight glasses of water between meals, relax whenever possible to reduce stress, and exercise daily.

Sorcerers in almost every country have methods for preventing diseases. Here are a few examples:

Ugandan natives wear around their necks a zango charm—a small piece of root decorated with animal skin, stones, or feathers.

In China, an amulet containing the eyelids of a frog and a kei stone is worn around the neck.

Italians chew raw garlic.

Jewish mothers make chicken soup for their families.

Romanian gypsies wear an amulet containing the eyes of newt.

Some Japanese wear surgical gauze masks over their faces when they appear in public.

During an epidemic, New England residents wear a string of asafetida around their necks.

Russian shamans prescribe birch bud tea twice daily.

In Mongolia and Turkestan, witch doctors prescribe panti (the powdered young horns of the royal spotted deer) infused in tea or vodka, as a drink.

Polish citizens sometimes wear bird bones in their clothes.

To prevent illness, *brujas* in Mexico hang *Ojos de Dios* (Eyes of God) yarn crosses in bedrooms.

Natives in New Guinea have been known to take the skull of a dead enemy, decorate it with stones and shells, and place it in their hut. If they don't have a real head, they substitute a coconut shell.

Proctitis

Inflammation of the rectal mucosa.

Primary Symptoms: Rectal discomfort, constipation, gas, and bloody mucus discharges. Often it is a form of ulcerative colitis.

Treatment: Balkan folk healers recommend local application of moist heat, and bed rest.

Prolapsis Ani

Symptoms: A protrusion of the mucous lining of the rectum.

Treatment: Mexican *brujas* oil a piece of muslin with olive oil. Then they apply it to the protrusion to soften it enough so it can be properly repositioned.

In Russia, if the protrusion is inflamed, shamans apply a poultice of slippery elm bark, and put the patient on a well-balanced diet, along with brown bread, mush, hasty pudding, Tiger's Milk, and molasses.

Prostatitis

An inflammation of the prostate gland.

Primary Symptoms: Pain and pressure around the gland, and frequent urinating that produces a burning sensation.

Treatment: Turkish shamans apply equal parts of iodine and belladonna to the affected area. Then they have the patient rest in bed with cold towels on his stomach, and have him take hot sitz baths three times daily.

Spanish gypsies feed their patients bee pollen, and put them on a special diet (see Chapter Four: Diets).

Pruritis

Symptoms: Itching.

Treatment: Curanderos in Peru apply a solution of borax and water to the affected area, and have the patient eat bananas with buttermilk.

Vermont folk practitioners apply apple cider vinegar to the skin six times daily.

Psoriasis

A chronic inflammatory skin ailment sometimes caused by a nervous condition.

Symptoms: Onset is usually gradual, and is characterized by pinhead-size spots with silver-white scales. There is seldom any itching.

Treatment: Hawaiian *kahunas* have their patients eat pineapple, but not at the same meal with cereals or starches.

New Zealand Maoris put their patients on a special diet of lamb with green vegetables, and sarsaparilla tea.

Ptomaine Poisoning
(Food Poisoning)

Primary Symptoms: Stomach cramps, nausea, and vomiting. (In botulism, the most dangerous and severe case of food poisoning, there is also weakness, paralysis, and difficulty in swallowing, talking, and seeing; often fatal.)

Prevention: Vermont folk practitioners, like other healers, advise refrigerating poultry dressing, seafood, pork, and mayonnaise. They warn against eating toadstools, tainted beans, and improperly home canned foods. They recommend avoiding the use of food from bulging, leaking, or rusty cans.

Tahitians sprinkle fish with lime juice before eating it.

Treatment: New England folk healers recommend drinking honey and vinegar for mild cases of food poisoning. (For severe cases of food poisoning, or for botulism, they advise going to a hospital for antitoxin therapy.)

Mexican *brujas* light two blue candles, and pass a brown egg over the patient's stomach. Then they put him on a special diet for poisoning (see Chapter Four: Diets), and later have him drink donkey's milk.

In New Guinea, the witch doctor spits on a banana, and has the patient eat it. Then he applies his blow pipe to the patient's stomach, and "sucks out" the evil spirits.

In Uganda, the *nganga* feeds the patient dry mustard and egg whites in warm water, and chants: *"Katui nui bomba."*

Purpura

A shortage of platelets in the blood, causing bleeding to occur spontaneously, particularly from the nose and in the mouth. Bleeding underneath the skin is frequent, giving the appearance of bruising.

Treatment: Gypsies in Spain feed their patients Barley Water, Egg-Lemonade (see Chapter Five: Health Recipes), egg whites (no egg yolks), milk, gelatin water, lemonade, orange juice, grape juice, and dry albumin in milk, along with fluellin herb tea twice daily.

Pyorrhea

A discharge of pus from the tooth socket along the side of the gum causing permanent injury to the gum and root.

Treatment: Cherokee Indian medicine men advise patients to brush their teeth and massage their gums well with goldenseal tea at least twice daily.

Brujas in Mexico rub their patients' gums with the rattle from a rattlesnake.

Russian shamans prescribe a 3 percent solution of peroxide as a mouthwash after each meal.

Pyrosis

Symptoms: Trickling saliva from the mouth, and stomach cramps.

Treatment: In India, gurus put the patient on a special diet (see Chapter Four: Diets), and feed him 1/2 teaspoon of salt in a glass of water twice daily.

Q Fever

An infectious disease which may be contracted by drinking raw milk from contaminated cows.

Primary Symptoms: Headache, chills, fever, profuse sweating, and slowness of heartbeat.

Treatment: Hawaiian *kahunas* feed patients Egg-Lemonade (see Chapter Five: Health Recipes), and call a medical specialist.

Quinsy

Abscess of tonsil capsule due to bacterial inflammation.

Primary Symptoms: Sore throat, pain in swallowing, redness and swelling of the tonsils, dry throat, foul tongue, hoarseness, difficulty in breathing, and a slight fever.

Treatment: Witch doctors in Borneo put the patient to bed, put him on a special diet (see Chapter Four: Diets), bathe his body twice daily, and bathe his feet in a tepid solution of mustard and water.

Navajo Indian medicine men have the patient drink goldenseal tea, with cayenne pepper in it, several times daily.

Russian shamans boil a handful of sage leaves in 2 pints of water with 1/2 pint of vinegar, and have the patient inhale the vapor.

Rabies
(Hydrophobia)

Causes: The bite, or the infection from saliva, of a rabid animal.

Symptoms: Mental depression, restlessness, malaise, fever, and swelling around the bite. Later there may be foaming at the mouth, great thirst, a morbid fear of water, convulsions, and death. If untreated before these symptoms begin, it is usually fatal.

Treatment: Vermont folk healers, as other healers do, generally advise when a person has been bitten by any animal, the animal should be confined and kept under observation for at least ten days to see if it is rabid. If the animal has rabies, they recommend the Pasteur treatment. Right away they may cleanse the bite with vinegar, and perhaps undertake the task of cauterizing it with a few drops of muriatic acid.

Traditional healers in Afghanistan have their patients drink xanthium tea four times daily.

Radiation Sickness

Symptoms: Loss of appetite, nausea, vomiting, anemia, and diarrhea due to overexposure to x-rays, or other radiation.

Treatment: Shamans in Japan have patients eat lemons.

Ramsay Hunt Syndrome

Invasion of the ear by the herpes zoster virus.

Primary Symptoms: Pain in the ear, loss of hearing, vertigo, chills, fever, malaise, gastrointestinal upsets, facial paralysis on the involved side, and vesicular eruptions in the external auditory canal.

Treatment: New England folk practitioners recommend a diet rich in vitamin B_{12} (see Chapter Six: Vitamins and Minerals), and sponge the rash with apple cider vinegar.

Brujas in Mexico pass a hard-boiled egg over the afflicted area, while burning incense and singing a special *icaro.*

Rat-Bite Fever

Causes: Bites of infected rats, or rat droppings in food.

Primary Symptoms: Swelling and inflammation of the lymph glands, chills, fever, and rigidity of body parts.

Treatment: In Malaysia, witch doctors wash rat bites

with vinegar, and sometimes use the following treatment
of cauterizing the wound with carbolic acid, and taking 3
handfuls of jimson leaves, adding 1 quart of boiling water, reducing it to a pint by boiling, straining it, and
having the patient drink one tablespoon twice daily.

Raynaud's Disease

Causes: The blocking of the small arteries arresting the
circulation of the blood in the body, especially to the
fingers and toes.

Symptoms: The affected parts turn white, waxy, and
numb, or swell, tingle, and turn purple. They may not
even bleed if pricked.

Treatment: African *ngangas* in Kenya advise patients to
stop smoking, keep warm, and massage their legs, arms,
and fingers. Then they place a piece of fox fur around
the patient's neck, burn St. Jude's incense, and sing this
incantation: "The wicked demon which seizes the body,
the bad wind by itself, Spirit of the heavens conjure it!
Spirit of the earth conjure it!"

Vermont folk practitioners recommend a diet rich in
Vitamin B_3 (see Chapter Six: Vitamins and Minerals).

Relapsing Fever

An infectious disease transmitted by ticks, lice, or
bedbugs.

Primary Symptoms: Recurrent attacks of high fever (105°
F. or more), headache, and weakness.

Treatment: Most folk healers recommend calling a medical specialist, especially when fever is high.

Australian witch doctors prescribe strict bed rest with
cool sponge baths. They have the patient drink tea made
from the root of the ironweed, 1/2 cupful three or four
times daily.

Retention of Urine

This malady has many causes, among them paralysis, injury, obstruction or inflammation of the bladder, kidney stones, tumors, or enlarged prostate glands.

Symptoms: Edema (swelling of the body tissues).

Treatment: Vermont folk healers prescribe the following, as natural diuretics: asparagus, cucumbers, cranberry juice, grapes, parsley, watercress, caraway seeds, and watermelon seed tea.

Shamans in Mongolia feed their patients pulverized egg shells, 1 teaspoon every hour.

Rheumatic Fever

Primary Symptoms: This disease often occurs as a complication of tonsillitis or sore throat, and is most common among young people. The temperature rises to 102° F. to 104° F.; and the pulse becomes rapid. There is profuse sweating, pain in the joints, swelling of the joints, and prostration. Sometimes there is a rash. The disease often reoccurs after it has apparently gone, and sometimes causes permanent damage to the heart or kidneys.

Treatment: Bavarian gypsies prescribe strict bed rest, and rose hips tea six times daily, along with a diet rich in vitamin C (see Chapter Six: Vitamins and Minerals). After the patient is well, they restrict him in his activities, especially any strenuous sports.

Rheumatism

Symptoms: There are several types of rheumatism, but the most common is the inflammation of joints, such as fingers, shoulder, elbow, or knee. The affected joints are swollen, tense, surrounded by a rose-colored blush, and often very painful.

Treatment: Hawaiian *kahunas* pound chili pepper seeds with sea salt, and rub this on the afflicted joints.

Persian shamans apply oil of camphor to the painful areas.

In Korea, healers have the patient wear a copper bracelet.

Australian witch doctors rub eucalyptus oil on the joints, and put the patient on a special diet (see Chapter Four: Diets).

Rickets

A vitamin deficiency condition in children that results in failure of the skeleton to develop as it should.

Symptoms: Children with this disease usually have extended stomachs, thin arms, thin legs, and poor posture.

Treatment: In India, the guru puts the child on a diet containing, as available, milk, eggs, cod liver oil, chicken, oatmeal, tuna, salmon, lamb, vegetables, bread, fruit, and Lime Water (see Chapter Five: Health Recipes), along with skullcap tea six times daily. He also has the patient get a maximum of fresh air and sunshine.

Ringworm

A highly contagious infection caused by a fungus; often spreading to the scalp and nails.

Symptoms: Ring-shaped vesicles, itching, pain, and scaling.

Treatment: Folk healers in Lebanon apply castor oil to the eruptions twice daily.

Persian shamans apply bruised nasturtium leaves.

Rocky Mountain Spotted Fever

An infectious disease caused by tick bites usually in the Rocky Mountain states.

Symptoms: Malaise, chills, loss of appetite, headache, severe pains in the back and muscles, flushed face, sensitive eyes, dry cough, red rash, and a high fever sometimes reaching 105° F.

Prevention: Vaccination.

Treatment: Indian medicine men in Colorado have their patients wear an owl's claw around their necks, and if possible, they consult with a medical doctor.

Scabies

Microscopic itch mites burrow under the skin, causing extreme itching that may lead to infection.

Symptoms: Numerous blisters, small lesions, and "burrows."

Treatment: Sangomas in South Africa melt together, at low temperature, petroleum jelly and 1 ounce of sulphur. Then they scrub the patient's skin with carbolic acid, and apply the ointment twice daily for one week.

Scarlet Fever

A contagious disease usually affecting children.

Primary Symptoms: Sore throat, red rash over the entire body, coated tongue, shivering, loss of appetite, headache, high fever, malaise, and great thirst.

Treatment: Hopi Indian medicine men in Arizona apply a hot bran poultice to the patient's throat, sponge his body with vinegar and water, and soak his hands and feet in hot mustard water. They recommend a special diet (see Chapter Four: Diets).

Traditional healers in Japan used to apply mashed raw cranberries to the rash.

In Haiti, voodootherapists treat this disease by adding 2 teaspoons cayenne pepper and 1 teaspoon salt to 1/2 pint of boiling water, letting the mixture stand for 16 minutes, then adding 1/2 pint of vinegar, and letting it stand for a half hour, then straining the mixture through a fine cloth, and feeding the patient 2 tablespoons every half hour.

Scars

Treatment: Canadian Indian medicine men in the Yukon marinate pine needles in alcohol for a week, and apply the liquid daily to the scars. Then they put the patient on a special diet (see Chapter Four: Diets).

Schistosomiasis

A parasitic disease due to infestation by organisms in polluted waters, notably the upper Nile River.
Primary Symptoms: High fever, dermatitis, cystitis, and chronic dysentery.
Treatment: Egyptian shamans feed the patient pumpkin seeds, and wild day lily tea; nothing else for 24 hours; however, if this doesn't cure the patient, they consult a medical specialist.

Sciatica

Symptoms: Severe pains in the back of the leg.
Treatment: Ancient Romans applied dry heat to the patient's leg, along with a liniment made from equal parts of olive oil and eucalyptus oil. Then they fed him one bud of raw garlic daily.
Polish shamans advise patients to wear long, red woolen underwear, and carry a raw beet in their pocket.

Scleroderma

A serious disease in which all the layers of skin become hard and rigid.
Primary Symptoms: The hands and feet turn blue, and then white or yellow.

Treatment: Mexican *brujas* wash the patient's skin with black soap to chase away the evil spirits.

Curanderos in Argentina apply an ointment of petroleum jelly and mashed cucumbers to the patient's skin, have him drink maté tea, and put him on a special diet (see Chapter Four: Diets).

Vermont folk practitioners advise patients to inhale the fumes of apple brandy from a charred oak keg four times daily.

Scorpion Sting

A very painful sting from an "insect" with an elongated body, eight legs, two pinchers, and a long tail. It stings with its tail, and the sting is often fatal.

Treatment: Mexican *brujas* apply the juice of the aloe vera plant to the sting, and if possible, send the patient to a clinic for antivenin therapy.

Scrofula
(King's Evil)

Primary Symptoms: This disease chiefly affects the glands, and is characterized by small kernels under the skin of the neck, and under the jaw. The remain for a long time, often gathering and breaking. The eyelids are often attacked, and become thickened and inflamed, discharging a thick mucus.

Prevention: In England, folk healers recommend drinking nettle tea twice daily.

Treatment: In Greece, shamans take a handful of walnut leaves, bruise, steep in a pint of water, strain, and sweeten with honey, giving the patient 1/3 of this quantity each day. Then they apply a poultice of bran and slippery elm to the tumors, and put the patient on a special diet (see Chapter Four: Diets). On the night of a full moon, they have a virgin spit on the patient three times, and say: "Apollo, let not the plague increase which a virgin has allayed."

Healers in Lapland advise moderate exercise in fresh air daily, and 1 tablespoon of cod liver oil twice daily.

Scurvy

Symptoms: This disease is common to those with a vitamin C deficiency. It is characterized by weariness, difficulty in breathing, rottenness and bleeding of the gums, difficulty in walking, bad breath, a falling away of the flesh of the legs on which there appear violet spots, a pale and leaden-colored face, scaly eruptions over the body, and dysentery.

Treatment: In England, folk healers prescribe eating limes.

Seasickness

Symptoms: This ailment is characterized by dizziness, nausea, and vomiting. It occurs on a boat in rough waters. The patient usually recovers when he reaches land.

Treatment: Hawaiian *kahunas* advise eating soda crackers, sucking a lemon, and applying a copper penny to the navel.

Sea Urchin Sting

Treatment: In Samoa, shamans apply a drop of hot wax to the sting.

Senility

Symptoms: This condition often occurs in people past middle age, and is characterized by absentmindedness, forgetfulness, and a lack of interest in anything.

Treatment: Chinese herbalists advise older people to get plenty of fresh air and exercise, and interest themselves in work or hobbies. They have them drink ginseng tea several times daily, and go on a special diet (see Chapter Four: Diets).

The *nganga* in Uganda places an amulet, in the shape of a phoenix bird, around the patient's neck, and coats his temples with the gall of a partridge.

Shingles

Primary Symptoms: Heat, itching, and tingling on some parts of the body with an eruption of transparent pimples that are filled with a clear fluid. The pimples finally run together, and turn black, terminating in thin dark scabs. After about fourteen days, they fall off.

Treatment: New England folk practitioners wet the pimples with apple cider vinegar, and feed the patient sassafras tea twice daily.

Shock

Symptoms: The patient feels faint due to trauma or an emotional upset, like being in an accident. He is pale and cold, has a feeble pulse, half-closed eyelids, and irregular breathing.

Treatment: Japanese folk healers place the patient on his back with feet raised. They loosen tight clothing, keep him warm, and rub his arms and legs. Then they summon medical help as the condition is often fatal.

Silicosis

Symptoms: This disease affects the lungs, and occurs among workers, especially miners, who constantly breathe silicon or graphite dust. The symptoms are slow to develop, and in advanced cases it is characterized by a dry cough, decreased chest expansion, chest pains, malaise, disturbed sleep, and hoarseness. There is usually no fever.

Treatment: Folk practitioners in Wales boil onions, put

them through a sieve, add honey, lemon juice, and whiskey, and give 1 tablespoon every 4 hours. They advise the patient to quit smoking, change occupations (or wear a mask), and move to a pollution-free environment. In his diet they include cereals, wheat germ, and salads of lettuce and raw vegetables.

Sinusitis
(Sinus Trouble)

Symptoms: Headache, pains on either side of the nose, and running of the nose and eyes.

Treatment: Vermont folk practitioners advise their patient to avoid tobacco and beer. They recommend chewing honeycomb, and eating rye bread with grape juice.

Skin Cleanser

In Turkey, beauticians, especially for blackheads, take ripe avocados, mash, and apply to the skin. They leave the mixture on for a few minutes, remove with tissue, and apply rose water.

Skin Infections

Symptoms: Painful red sores containing pus.

Treatment: Haitian *houngas* apply white sugar to the infection, and then put the patient on a special diet (see Chapter Four: Diets).

Brujas in Mexico kill a snake that is not angry, skin it, toast it over a fire, cut it up, and put it in the patient's food.

Sleeping Sickness
(Trypanosomiasis or Chaga's Disease)

Causes: This disease is caused by the bite of the tsetse fly which is usually found in Africa, but sometimes in

South America. It differs from other flies notably in that it has crossed wings.

Symptoms: Irregular fever, painful swelling, tremors, headache, apathy, and sleepiness. If convulsions develop, death soon follows.

Treatment: South African *sangomas* bathe their patients with a mixture of walnut leaves and water, and have them see a medical specialist.

In Zimbabwe, the *nganga* takes the bark and root of the *munanga* tree, and the root of the *murovapasi* tree, grinds them to a powder, and mixes it in the patient's porridge. He then places an amulet around the patient's neck containing the eyes of a nightingale.

Sleep Walking

Treatment: Vermont folk healers suggest sleep walkers place a pan of water by their beds so they can step in it, and wake up.

Smoking

To stop smoking, Chinese herbalists recommend magnolia bark tea.

Snake Bite

Prevention: Medicine men in Panama advise hikers to wear boots, and to wear a piece of jet stone around their necks.

Treatment: South African *sangomas*, as well as other healers, suggest to those who are bitten by a snake to kill it to determine if it is poisonous, and if it is, go to the hospital for antivenin therapy.

The *nganga* in Zimbabwe first uses a treatment now generally outmoded in Western medicine: applying a tourniquet above the bite, making two incisions at the bite, and sucking out the poison with a cupping horn. Next, he applies bruised plaintain leaves to the wound and gives the patient a little whiskey to drink.

Gurus in India advise patients to chew a piece of Indian snakeroot, and apply the residue to the bite.

Soldier's Heart
(Asthenia)

Symptoms: Breathlessness, giddiness, mental and physical fatigue, chest pains, and palpitations of the heart.

Canadian Indian medicine men feed their patients sesame seeds, and 1/4 teaspoon of cayenne pepper in a cup of water each day. They put him on a well-balanced diet, and often suggest he go fishing in a canoe to avoid stress.

Sore Throat

Treatment: Folk healers in Nova Scotia chop up a raw onion, put it in an old sock, and tie it around the sore neck.

Spear Wounds

Treatment: Apache Indian medicine men tell their patients to find the spear, and put it in a cool place. Then they apply smoked wool to the wound, and have the patient drink brandy.

Spermatorrhea

Symptoms: Involuntary seminal emissions.
Treatment: Vermont folk healers have the patient sleep on a hard bed, rise early, work hard, exercise often, and take cold showers. They advise he avoid undue sexual stimulation such as pornographic literature.

Chinese herbalists place a topaz around the patient's neck, and sprinkle his food with the powdered heart of a turtle.

Spider Bites

Symptoms: From poisonous spiders, such as the black widow, there may be severe pain at the bite, abdominal cramps, weakness, tremor, labored breathing and speech, excruciating pain in the limbs, paralysis, stupor, and delirium. If convulsions develop, death may soon follow.

Treatment: West African *guerisseurs*, like Western healers, advise patients to go to a hospital for antivenin and other therapy.

The *nganga* in Uganda ties a tourniquet for a brief interval above the bite, makes an incision, and sucks out the poison with a cupping horn. Then he applies bruised catnip leaves, and feeds the patient catnip tea.

Spine Injuries

Treatment: Maoris in New Zealand apply chopped raw onions to the back of the patient's neck.

Splinters

Treatment: Italian shamans apply Venice turpentine to the splinter to draw it out. For small splinters, they apply adhesive tape; then rip the tape off rapidly. For steel splinters, such as particles of steel wool, they remove them with a magnet.

In Russia, shamans apply tar to splinters for 20 minutes.

Mexican *brujas* fry beef kidney fat with chopped onions, and add twelve sow bugs. When it's cool, they knead it with their hands, and apply it to the splinter.

Spotted Fever

Symptoms: Violent pains in the stomach, head, joints, and limbs; or sometimes pain in a single toe or finger. Often the patient becomes totally blind or deaf. Bleedings are frequent from different parts of the body. A clay-like coldness comes over the whole system with a feeling of ice melting in the stomach. There is difficulty in swallowing, nausea, and vomiting. If the patient lives through this, purple spots and fever appear.

Treatment: Aside from calling for medical help, Australian witch doctors promote perspiration by feeding the patient brandy in water. Then they rub his back with brandy and cayenne pepper, and apply a hot water bottle to his feet.

Navajo Indian medicine men feed their patients pleurisy root tea several times daily, sponge them with vinegar and water, and bathe their feet in mustard and water. Then they apply a Mustard Plaster (see Chapter Five: Health Recipes) to the back of the patient's neck, and give him tincture of jamborandi, 20 drops every 3 hours.

Sprains

Symptoms: The sprained member is red, painful, and usually swollen.

Treatment: Healers in Japan use a common treatment. They place an ice pack on the sprained member, and elevate it. Then they apply a strong liniment, and bind the sprain with a semi-elastic bandage. If possible, they have it x-rayed to see if there are any broken bones.

In Afghanistan, sorcerers place a leather strap from a horse's harness around the patient's wrist.

Spring Fever

Symptoms: Lassitude and fatigue thought to be due to a change of season or weather.

Treatment: Folk practitioners in Nova Scotia give their patients sulphur and molasses, and sassafras tea to drink.

Sprue
(Celiac Disease)

A chronic intestinal disorder.

Primary Symptoms: Diarrhea, loss of weight, inflammation of the mouth, a sore red tongue, a swollen abdomen, and stomach cramps.

Treatment: Ngangas in Kenya have their patients go on a gluten-free diet (see Chapter Four: Diets), and wear an amulet containing the wings of a hummingbird.

Mexican *brujas* have their patients drink mullein leaf tea.

Starvation

Symptoms: Dark sunken eyes, bony arms and legs, and an extended stomach. Sometimes the patient is unconscious from lack of food.

Treatment: Gurus in India feed the patient warm milk, a drop at a time. The next day, they give him Beef Tea (see Chapter Five: Health Recipes), and chicken broth. They feed him often, but just a teaspoon at a time. Later they put him on a bland diet, with no meat or vegetables, until recovered.

Sterility

Ju-ju men in Togo, Africa prescribe the stone from the gizzard of an ostrich ground to a powder, and mixed in wine to drink.

Childless couples in Asia drink ginseng tea for fertility.

In Australia, aborigines wear the image of a crescent moon, or the claws of a crab around their necks.

Maoris in New Zealand wear tiki god charms.

Hawaiian *kahunas* recommend necklaces of boar's tusks.

In Mongolia, women drink koumis (fermented mare's milk).

Ugandan *ngangas* have their patients carry a piece of mugwort in a red silk bag decorated with feathers, and chant this incantation: *"Tooam te artemsia, ne lassus sim in via."*

English folk healers prescribe that couples burn red candles before retiring, and drink sarsaparilla tea.

Mexican *brujas* place the foot of a badger under the bed.

Stiff Neck

Treatment: Cherokee Indian medicine men give patients the juice of 1/2 lemon to drink twice daily, and rub lemon juice on their necks.

Stingray Stings

Prevention: When swimming, or skin diving, in warm sea water, watch out for stingrays—big, round flat fish with long skinny tails. They usually stay along the ocean floor.

Treatment: Brujas in Mexico apply *yerba de la raya* leaves—a plant which grows along the shore line in Mexico.

In Hawaii, *kahunas* apply hot vinegar to the sting.

Stomachache

Treatment: In England, folk healers have their patients drink peppermint tea.

Vermont folk practitioners recommend drinking 1 tablespoon of honey and 1 tablespoon of vinegar in a cup of hot water.

Marabouts in Senegal prescribe coring and shredding apples, adding honey and cinnamon, and eating them slowly with a spoon.

A ju-ju man in the northern part of the Ivory Coast, Africa.

A New Guinea witch doctor outside his office.

The author in a *bruja's* costume with a rattle and an *Ojo de Dios*.

A high priestess in Ghana.

A *nganga* in Uganda.

An Australian witch doctor.

In Australia, the witch doctor counteracts
a spell of a patient being "sung to death."

A *N'Doep* ceremony in Rufisque, Senegal.

An open-air pharmacy in Lome, Togo where
everything from a rattlesnake's rattle to
rhinoceros' horns can be purchased.

Some witch doctors like to advertise.

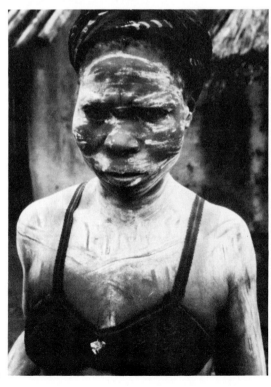

A patient at a *N'Doep* ceremony.

Marabout Sané
with a patient.

Marabout Djamyl Sané, Casamance, Senegal.

Anadi Faye, *guerisseur* (traditional healer) Dakar, Senegal.

A *curandero* in Oaxaca, Mexico.

The *curandero's* office.

Chinese sorcerers place jade amulets around their patient's neck, and sprinkle powdered jade in jasmine tea for him to drink.

Stomach Cramps

Prevention: Maoris in New Zealand advise eating slowly, and not swimming for an hour after eating.

Treatment: Aborigine sorcerers in Australia feed patients a cup of hot water with a tablespoon of sugar in it, and have them wear rabbit bones around their necks.

Stomach Wall Lacerations

Treatment: If there is internal bleeding with vomiting of blood, Russian shamans will of course consult a medical specialist. Meanwhile, they feed their patient shepherd's purse tea, and give his stomach a complete rest from food for a while. When the patient is better, they have him take long walks, and suck lemons sprinkled with sugar.

Strains

Symptoms: If the muscles, or ligaments, are strained, there is pain, redness, and sometimes swelling.

Treatment: Brujas in Mexico apply warm camphorated oil to the painful parts. If a lump appears, they fry a piece of pork fat, add 1 teaspoon of camomile tea, 1 cup of tequila, and 1 cup of vinegar. They boil this concoction, and apply it fairly hot to the lump.

Strep Throat

A throat infection caused by streptococcal bacteria.

Primary Symptoms: The throat is extremely sore and inflammed, and there is great difficulty in swallowing.

Treatment: Bavarian shamans hang a string of asafetida around the patient's neck, and have him eat lemons, gargle 1 teaspoon of vinegar in a glass of water several times daily, and feed him a cup of gold tea six times daily.

Stroke
(Apoplexy)

Symptoms: Abrupt loss of consciousness due to brain hemorrhage.

Treatment: In Mongolia, sorcerers call for medical assistance. They also apply Mustard Plasters (see Chapter Five: Health Recipes) to the soles of the patient's feet, apply wet salt to his head and temples, bind cords around his thighs, and when he regains consciousness, feed him a little salt water. Then they put him on a special diet (see Diet for Apoplexy in Chapter Four: Diets).

Stuttering

Treatment: In ancient Greece, therapists advised stutterers to read aloud for 2 hours each day, and Demosthenes at least, practiced speaking with pebbles in his mouth.

In Rome, stutterers practiced speaking while holding a small piece of wood between their front teeth.

Summer Complaint

Symptoms: Diarrhea in infants due to improper food, or to sour milk. It occurs most frequently in hot weather.

Treatment: Mexican *brujas* boil geranium roots in milk, and sweeten them with sugar, giving the patient 1/2 cupful three times daily.

Sunburn

Prevention: Hawaiian *kahunas* recommend coconut oil as a sun lotion, and, as others do, advise those with fair skin to sun themselves not more than 15 minutes at a time.

Treatment: Indians in Nantucket rub cider vinegar on sunburn.

Sunstroke

Symptoms: Face is red, perspiration is profuse, pulse is rapid, breathing deep, pupils of the eye are dilated, and there are severe cramping pains in the abdomen, arms, or legs.

Treatment: Turkish shamans sponge the patient's head with cold water, place him on his back with head and shoulders raised, and put Mustard Plasters (see Chapter Five: Health Recipes) on his legs. If possible, they call a medical specialist, and upon recovery, don't allow him malt, beer, or liquor.

Swellings

Treatment: Witch doctors in Lapland warm a reindeer's foot, and rub it over the swelling. Then they apply the bruised leaves of the chervil plant.

For swollen ankles, Irish folk practitioners apply grated raw potatoes.

Syphilis

A venereal disease caused by sexual contact with infected persons. It can also be passed to a fetus in pregnancy.

Symptoms: At first, sores, of a brassy or copperish color, on the sex organs and around the mouth.

Treatment: In Italy, shamans feed patients grapes, and plantain tea three times daily.

South African *sangomas* prescribe 1 tablespoon of raw potato juice every 2 hours; however, if the patient does not improve, he consults with a Western doctor for antibiotics, such a penicillin.

Tarantula Bites

Treatment: Sorcerers in Iraq soak matches in hot water for 30 minutes, and apply this solution to a bite.

In Mongolia, shamans make a serum by placing three live tarantulas in hot olive oil for three weeks. The oil is then strained, and applied to a bite once every hour.

Teething

When babies are cutting teeth, they cry constantly.

Treatment: Ngangas in Uganda make a necklace of spiderwort seed pods, and hang it around the baby's neck.

Folk practitioners in Ireland rub a small amount of whiskey on the baby's gums, and give him a rubber ring to chew on.

Tetanus

Primary Symptoms: Lockjaw, fever, convulsions, and sore throat.

Prevention: Vaccination is good for three years.

Treatment: New England folk practitioners apply a piece of salt pork to puncture wounds for several hours, or overnight, believing this will draw out the spores which cause this disease.

Turkish shamans apply tobacco to the chest, armpits, and stomach. If the patient does not improve, they call a medical specialist as the disease is often fatal.

Thrush

Symptoms: A sore mouth usually in infants.

Treatment: Shamans in Russia wash out the baby's mouth with a weak solution of borax and water three times daily.

Tick Bites

An insect which attaches itself firmly to an animal, or person, and sucks blood.

Treatment: In Pakistan, witch doctors put 2 or 3 drops of chloroform on the tick, and cup the hand over it for 1 minute.

Tinnitis

Symptoms: Loud or ringing noises in the ear.
Treatment: Persian shamans heat summer savory with a little oil of roses, and put 1 or 2 drops of it in the ear.

Tonsillitis

An inflammation of the tonsils.
Symptoms: Sore throat, fever, redness of throat and palate, yellowish secretions on the swollen tonsils, and headache.
Treatment: Ngangas in Zimbabwe advise the patient to stay in bed while ill, and be on a special diet (see Chapter Four: Diets). They have him gargle 1 teaspoon of baking soda in a glass of warm water, and keep cold compresses on his throat. When three successive attacks occur within three years, or in any one serious case, the *nganga* advises consulting a medical specialist.

Curanderos in Colombia mix coffee grounds with lard and sesame oil, and apply it to the soles of the patient's feet.

Hawaiian *kahunas* mix sap from a raw sweet potato with warm water for the patient to gargle.

Toothache

Treatment: If a filling falls out of a tooth, *ngangas* in Kenya make a temporary filling from a piece of chewing gum, or some melted wax, and send the patient to a dentist if possible.

A universal folk remedy is to apply oil of cloves to the tooth.

Gypsies in Yugoslavia seep the tooth in brandy, and then rub it with the middle toe of an owl while chanting: *"Galbes, galbat, galdes, galdat."*

Tooth Decay

Prevention: Mexican *brujas* recommend brushing the teeth, after each meal, with baking soda and salt, eating a minimum of candy (especially cactus candy), and eating an apple a day. For excessive tartar on the teeth, they advise eating strawberries.

Natives in Burma chew beetle nut to prevent tooth decay.

Arctic eskimos chew whale blubber.

Natives in Zimbabwe rub their teeth with *gariko* root.

In Samoa, children eat cashew nuts for better teeth.

Treatment: For children's baby teeth, English folk healers advise pulling them if they are decayed. True to folklore they tie a string to a door knob, and tie the other end of the string to the child's tooth, then slam the door. They tell the child to sing: "Big rat, little rat, here's my old tooth, pray give me a new one." The child puts his old tooth under the pillow so the tooth fairies will take it, and leave him some money.

Toxemia

Symptoms: This ailment occurs in pregnant women, and is characterized by excessive weight gain and swelling, headache, drowsiness, weakness, and high blood pressure.

Treatment: Voodootherapists in Haiti put the patient on a low-salt diet (see Chapter Four: Diets). Also, he has her drink Voodoo Brew (see Chapter Five: Health Recipes), white wine, and goat's milk.

Toxoplasmosis

Primary Symptoms: High fever, swollen glands, aching joints, weakness, and sore eyes.

Prevention: Vermont folk practitioners offer the common sense to not eat raw or undercooked meat or poultry. They also advise washing one's hands after handling a cat's litter box as this parasite is common to the intestinal tract of cats.

Treatment: South African *sangomas* put the patient on a diet for typhoid fever (see Chapter Four: Diets), have him stay in bed, and if he becomes worse, they call a medical specialist.

Trench Mouth

Symptoms: A contagious sore mouth spread by kissing or other close contact, or by drinking out of contaminated glasses.

Treatment: English folk healers advise rinsing out the mouth, several times daily, with a weak solution of peroxide and water.

Trichinosis

Causes: Eating raw or undercooked pork.

Primary Symptoms: Swelling of the upper eyelids, muscular pains, high fever, thirst, profuse sweating, hemorrhaging, weakness, prostration, and difficulty in swallowing.

Treatment: Since the disease is often fatal, South African *sangomas* advise calling a medical specialist.

Shamans in Russia give their patients shepherd's purse tea, alternated with clove tea, to drink. Then they apply cold compresses to his eyelids, and anoint his skin with fresh eel oil.

To alleviate the pain, the African *nganga* in the Congo rubs the patient's muscles with the marrow from a hyena's bone.

Tuberculosis

Primary Symptoms: Chest pains, weight loss, and the coughing up of sputum. The disease is very contagious.

Treatment: Folk practitioners in Nova Scotia have their patients inhale the fumes of apple brandy from a charred oak keg four times daily, and refer the patient to a medical specialist for treatment.

South American *brujas* along the Amazon River give their patients the juice from the bark of a banana tree, goat's milk, and raw eggs in beer.

Tularemia

Causes: This disease is caused by rabbit bites, or from eating or handling wild rabbits, and is named after Tulare, California.

Symptoms: Headache, chills, high fever, vomiting, weakness, drenching sweats, and ulcers, especially in the mouth and eye.

Treatment: Ngangas in Nigeria recommend strict bed rest, and a bland diet of Magic Protein Potion, Zango Mango, Nganga Banana Shakes, and Arrowroot Water (see Chapter Five: Health Recipes).

South African *sangomas* usually consult a medical specialist about administering antibiotics as the disease is often fatal.

Tumors

An abnormal mass or swelling. If it increases in size, it might be malignant.

Treatment: Witch doctors in Turkey boil figs in milk, and apply it to the lump for three or four days. If it is benign, it may disappear; but if not, they call a cancer specialist.

Tympanites

Primary Symptoms: Hardened swelling of the abdomen which when thumped sounds like a drum; great thirst, loss of appetite, pain in the loins, rumbling of the stomach, and constipation.

Treatment: Ngangas in Zimbabwe massage the patient's stomach, and apply a hot bran poultice to it. Then they put him on a special diet (see Chapter Four: Diets), and have him drink a cup of senna tea several times daily, and if the patient does not rapidly improve, they consult a medical specialist.

Typhoid Fever

A disease transmitted by flies, contaminated water or milk.

Primary Symptoms: Chills, high fever, rose-colored spots on the chest and abdomen, backache, sore throat, falling hair, delirium, hot body with cold extremities, weakness, headache, deafness, bad breath, twitching of the tendons, hemorrhaging, and dry tongue. If the patient lives through this, he is generally immune for life.

Prevention: Cherokee Indians suck lemons to prevent this disease, but they also utilize vaccination.

Treatment: Haitian *houngans* recommend strict bed rest, and a special diet (see Chapter Four: Diets).

Folk healers in England put a poultice of tansy leaves on the patient's stomach.

Russian shamans feed the patient 10 drops of spirits of turpentine on a lump of sugar twice daily. If possible, they call a medical specialist as the disease is often fatal.

Typhus

Primary Symptoms: This disease, caused by tick bites, is characterized by loss of strength, delirium, spasms in various parts of the body, nausea, red gums, crusted teeth, swollen tongue, swollen abdomen, weak and irregular pulse, insomnia, red spots on the skin, and high fever.

Prevention: Vaccination is good for six years.

Treatment: New England folk practitioners advise strict bed rest, a bland diet, and hard apple cider. Since the disease is often fatal, they also consult a medical specialist.

Ulceration of the Womb

Primary Symptoms: A sensation of rawness, burning, and smarting in the womb, pain in the right side of the abdomen, pain in the back of the neck, pain on top of the head, and leukorrhea.

Treatment: Women shamans in Russia tell the patient to drink unicorn root tea, and then boil the root of the white pond lily in water, cool it, and inject the liquid into the vagina twice daily.

Hungarian gypsies have their patients drink camomile tea.

Ulcers

Primary Symptoms: Burning and swelling of the stomach which is relieved after eating, but then begins again after a few hours when the stomach is empty. Often there is vomiting.

Treatment: Hungarian gypsies put their patients on a special diet (see Chapter Four: Diets), and have them drink raw cabbage juice as their only drink.

Vermont folk healers suggest patients take 1/2 pound of brewer's yeast in water 1 hour before breakfast, drink buttermilk between meals, practice transcendental meditation, and take a long relaxing vacation.

For external ulcers (sores that don't heal), or sores which excrete pus, *ngangas* in Kenya boil walnut leaves, add a small amount of sugar, and apply it to the sore nightly. During the day, they fan the sore with walnut leaves, and sing this *icaro*:

"That which does not go away, bad ulcers,
Poignant ulcers, enlarged ulcers, perforated ulcers,
Ulcers which spread, benign ulcers, malignant ulcers,

Spirits of the earth conjure it!
Spirits of the heavens conjure it!"

Undulant Fever
(Brucellosis, Malta Fever, or Gibraltar Fever)

Cause: This disease is caused by drinking raw milk from contaminated cows.

Primary Symptoms: Remittent fever, malaise, pain, constipation, sweating, and weakness.

Treatment: Vermont folk healers recommend strict bed rest, Beef Tea (see Chapter Five: Health Recipes), and lemonade. Since the disease is often fatal, they usually consult a medical specialist about administering drugs.

Uremia

The retention of urine due to a toxic condition poisoning the system.

Primary Symptoms: Weakness, malaise, bad breath, and body odor.

Treatment: Shamans in Poland consult doctors, and have the patient drink garlic juice in hot milk with 1 teaspoon of honey, twice daily.

Cherokee Indian medicine men have their patients drink Corn Silk Tea (see Chapter Five: Health Recipes), and cranberry juice. In their diet they include asparagus, watercress, watermelon, and cucumbers.

Vaginitis
(Infection of the Vagina)

Symptoms: Frequent urination, and an odoriferous discharge from the vagina.

Prevention: Women should cleanse themselves properly after using the bathroom, wiping from front to back.

Treatment: Women shamans, in Russia, prescribe taking a hot bath with 1 cup of salt in the bath water, and then inserting freshly made acidophilus yogurt into the vagina at bedtime.

Valley Fever
(Posada-Wernicke's Disease)

A highly infectious fungus disease occurring mainly in California's San Joaquin Valley, and in some parts of South America.

Primary Symptoms: Chills, fever, cough, chest pains, sputum, sore throat, a rash, a respiratory infection, and the coughing up of blood (hemoptysis).

Treatment: The disease is often fatal; therefore, patients in California usually call for the aid of a physician who, among other things, usually prescribes antibiotics.

Curanderos in Bolivia may also call for medical aid, prescribe complete bed rest, and have the patient breathe steam from boiling citrus leaves. For the rash, they apply a hot paste made from 1/2 ounce of brown soap, 2 ounces of roasted onions, 1 1/2 ounce of ground mustard, and 2 ounces of sugar. For hemoptysis, they have the patient drink bugleweed tea several times daily.

Varicose Veins

Symptoms: Protruding purple veins in the legs.

Treatment: Vermont folk practitioners apply apple cider vinegar to the veins nightly, and massage the patient's legs frequently. They recommend regular exercise daily.

Vomiting

Treatment: Shamans in Singapore wring out a cloth in cold water, and apply it to the patient's neck. Then they place a Mustard Plaster (see Chapter Five: Health Recipes) on his stomach, and feed him cascarilla bark tea several times daily.

Warts

Symptoms: Small "bumps," especially on the fingers, containing "seeds."

Treatment: Bulgarian gypsies have the patient steal a dish rag, and apply castor oil to the wart twice daily, often making it disappear in about three or four weeks.

Persian shamans recommend a special diet (see Chapter Four: Diets).

Wasp Stings

Treatment: In Japan and elsewhere, folk healers advise patients who are allergic to wasp stings, or who are stung by a large number of them, to get medical help quickly, as a bad reaction can be fatal.

New England folk practitioners apply vinegar to the sting.

Navajo Indian medicine men rub the sting with a slice of lemon.

Wen
(Cyst)

Symptoms: A benign tumor, composed of fatty matter, that is smooth and movable, and enclosed in a sac beneath the skin.

Treatment: Mexican *brujas* take the yolk of an egg, beat it up, and add as much salt as will dissolve; then they apply this to the wen every 12 hours.

White Swelling

Symptoms: This disease occurs mostly in children, and is characterized where the hip, or another joint, is inflamed while the skin remains white. There is usually great pain and swelling.

Treatment: Shamans in Russia boil the root of

bearsfoot, mix it with lard, and apply it to the swollen part three times daily. Then they cover it with a piece of flannel ironed with a hot iron.

Whooping Cough

This disease appears frequently in small children, and is generally preceded by a cold.

Primary Symptoms: Coughing with a characteristic whoop.

Treatment: The African *nganga* in Kenya recommends strict bed rest, a special diet (see Chapter Four: Diets), and chestnut leaf tea several times daily.

Worms

Symptoms: A coated tongue with red "pimples" on the sides of it. Often there is diarrhea and there may be vomiting of worms, the skin is grayish with a lead-colored semi-circle under they eyes, there may be an increase in appetite, the face is puffy, the patient loses weight, and the abdomen may become enlarged and swollen.

Treatment: Spanish gypsies feed their patients nothing but pulverized raw pumpkin seeds in milk for 24 hours.

For all types of worms, even tapeworm, Persian shamans feed their patients nothing but pomegranates for 24 hours.

For dracunculiasis, worms appearing in ulcers on the skin, shamans in Pakistan apply garlic juice to the ulcers, and have the patient eat garlic—one bud daily.

Wounds

Treatment: Mexican *brujas* stop the bleeding first, and then cleanse the wound with alcohol or tequila. Next they apply iodine, or betadine, let it dry, and bandage with sterile gauze. For internal wounds, they crush the leaf of the maguey cactus, boil the juice, and have the patient drink it.

Maoris in New Zealand apply rata wine to wounds, and put the patient on a special diet (see Chapter Four: Diets).

Wrinkles
(Xeroderma)

Treatment: Hawaiian *kahunas* in Niihau mix 1 ounce of coconut oil with 1/4 ounce of almond oil, and apply it to the skin, massaging upwards.

Yaws

A highly contagious disease occurring mainly in rural communities in hot, moist climates.

Primary Symptoms: Sores on the face, neck, and arms; pains in the limbs, headache, loss of appetite, chills, and fever.

Treatment: The African *nganga* in Ghana treats the sores with an elm bark poultice. Then he has the patient drink sassafras tea, or dandelion tea, several times daily.

Yellow Fever

An acute infectious disease transmitted by the bite of infected mosquitoes in tropical areas.

Primary Symptoms: Severe pain in the limbs, high fever, nausea, vomiting (often black), red and watery eyes, red tongue, jaundice, sore stomach with burning pains, headache, hurried breathing, sore throat, flushed face, and a disturbed mind.

Prevention: Vaccination is good for ten years.

Ju-ju men on the Ivory Coast of West Africa hang sweet clover in a room to ward off mosquitoes.

Treatment: Since this disease is often fatal, South African *sangomas* suggest consulting a medical specialist. In the meantime, they have the patient maintain strict bed rest, and put him on a liquid diet (see Chapter Four: Diets), with no solid food until completely recovered.

Sorcerers in Morocco have their patients drink copious amounts of orange blossom tea.

South American *curanderos* along the Amazon River mix a tumblerful of olive oil with the juice of three limes and salt, 1 tablespoon every 2 hours.

In Zimbabwe, for the fever, the *nganga* splits two white herrings, and applies them to the soles of the patient's feet.

CHAPTER FOUR

Diets

Listed below are some diets utilized by various traditional healers, and nutritional therapists, for general information only. Consult your own physician, or nutritionist, for advice pertaining to any particular diet in your special case.

Diet for Acidity

Eat: Buckwheat cakes with honey, cereals, red wine with dark bread between meals, chicken, fish, lamb, green vegetables, corn bread, pineapple juice, rhubarb, prunes, berries, black coffee, and orange marmalade.

Avoid: Bananas, raw apples, egg whites, fatty and fried foods, starchy vegetables with meats, and carbonated beverages.

Diet for Acne

Eat: Meat, milk, whole grain cereals, green vegetables, carrots, alfalfa sprouts, watercress, cabbage, egg yolks, wheat germ, cheddar cheese, yeast, cole slaw, yogurt, rice, and celery.

Avoid: Sweets, fish, shellfish, and carbonated beverages.

Diet for Alzheimer's Disease

Eat: 6 glasses of skim milk per day, stuffed baked potatoes, pompano en papillote, fillet of sole Florentine, iguana, red snapper, oysters Rockefeller, ceviche, scampi, tuna, trout, salmon, salads, spinach, chicken soup, raw vegetables, fresh pineapple, asparagus, and oatmeal with bananas and lecithin.

Avoid: Baking powder, non-dairy creamer, cake or pancake mix, frozen dough, processed cheese, buffered aspirin, anti-diarrhea products, and alcoholic beverages.

Diet for Anemia

Eat: Liver Tonic Mrewa, Magic Protein Potion, Nganga Banana Shakes, Voodoo Brew, Whazi Wizi, Witch Doctor's Potion, Zulu Brew (see Chapter Five: Health Recipes), green vegetables, yeast, rare roast beef, steak, mushrooms, red wine and dark bread, almonds, egg yolks, apricots, lamb, heart, fish, shellfish, turkey, brown rice, wheat germ, parsley, prunes, raisins, liver, dry milk, gelatin, raw vegetables, black coffee, and tea.

Avoid: Fried foods, sweets, and carbonated beverages.

Diet for Apoplexy *(Stroke)*

Eat: Chicken soup, baked potatoes, mixed green salad, custard, cream soup, cream of wheat, rice, summer squash and pudding.

Avoid: Salmon, seafood, fried foods, meat, hot breads, white bread, raw apples, rhubarb, pastries, ice cream, pickles, or beef tea.

Diet for Arthritis

Eat: Oatmeal with bananas and non-dairy creamer, fish, shellfish, chicken, chicken soup, pineapple juice (every morning), grape juice, vegetable juice, raw vegetables, avocados, spinach, sunflower seeds, oysters Rockefeller, beets, dates, berries, dried fruit, soy beans, margarine, brussels sprouts, string beans, rice, carrots, wheat bread with no preservatives, squash, lamb, honey, corn oil, tea, and coffee.

Avoid: Red meat, duck, goose, veal, pork, wild game, fried foods, preserves, hot breads, dairy products, fresh water fish, lemons, pepper, dry roasted nuts, yams, potatoes, monosodium glutamate, chocolate, turnips, rutabaga, tomatoes, sweets, and alcoholic or carbonated beverages.

Diet for Assimilation (Poor)

Eat: Whazi Wizi (see Chapter Five: Health Recipes), milk, egg yolks, honey, salt, meat, chicken, fish, shellfish, peanut butter, peanut oil, red wine with dark bread, salads, vegetables (but not at the same time with fruit), and tea.

Avoid: Fried foods, beer, liquor, and carbonated beverages.

Diet for Athlete's Foot

Eat: Lamb, chicken, meat, green vegetables, salads, nuts, and shellfish.

Avoid: Fruit and beer.

Diet for Biliousness

Eat: Corn chowder, salads, spinach, chicken, zucchini, peas, summer squash, fruit juice, roast beef, lamb, and watermelon.

Avoid: Fried and fatty foods, pears, peaches, cantaloupe, potatoes, spices, pancakes, beans, turnips, kale, cabbage, pickles, hot breads, pastries, and liquor.

Diet for Cancer

Eat: Carrot Tonic, Egg-Lemonade, Arrowroot Water, Rice Water, Meigg's Food, Nganga Banana Shakes, Whazi Wizi, Witch Doctor's Potion, voodoo Brew, Violet Wafers (see Chapter Five: Health Recipes), beets (almost daily), brown rice, almonds, violets, soy beans, gelatin salads, sauerkraut, organically grown vegetables, fruit juice, bread without preservatives, oatmeal with honey, yogurt, figs, white chicken meat, white fish, roast lamb, herb teas, white wine, champagne, parfait d'amour, broccoli, raisin bran, collard greens, carrots, yams, spinach, kale, Swiss chard, squash, and canteloupe.

Avoid: Fried foods, red meats, barbecued spareribs, burned or charred meats, reheated fats, warmed up left-overs, cabbage, spicy foods, pork, bacon, chicken livers, dark meat, sugar, pastries, candy, beans, pickles, popcorn, potato chips, donuts, hot dogs, egg yolks, peanuts, dairy products, coffee, tea (except herb tea), coarse fruits and vegetables (such as rhubarb and celery), beer, hard liquor, and all processed foods.

Diet for Chorea *(St. Vitus' Dance)*

Eat: Fruits, cereals, green vegetables, cream, milk, eggs, boiled rice, chicken, and white fish.

Avoid: Fried foods, spicy foods, red meats, bulky food, coarse vegetables, pickles, sweets, tea, and coffee.

Diet for Colitis

Eat: Papaya Tea (see Chapter Five: Health Recipes), papaya, avocados, baked apples, baked potatoes, vegetables, eggs, grape juice, whole wheat or rye bread, dry milk, spinach, seafood, and herb teas.

Avoid: Fried foods, spicy food, coarse food, celery, lettuce, pineapple, raisins, beans, cabbage, prunes, rhubarb, cucumbers, cow's milk, peanuts, berries, tomatoes, seeds, melons, and coconut.

Diet for Constipation

Eat: Coconut Prune Cocktail (see Chapter Five: Health Recipes), bran flakes, prunes, rhubarb, figs, raisins, wheat germ, soy sauce, fruit, meat salads, licorice, pumpkin, olive oil, whole wheat bread, avocados, and fresh raspberries.

Avoid: Blackberries, cheese, white rice, white bread, fried foods, apples, pickles, spicy foods, nuts, and barley.

Diet for Cystitis

Eat: Chicken, rice, nut bread, whole wheat bread, prunes, beets, string beans, peas, lettuce, and milk toast.

Avoid: Tomatoes, onions, spinach, cabbage, brussels sprouts, cauliflower, sorrel, green peppers, citrus fruit, pears, apples, spicy dishes, strawberries, currants, kidneys, soups, butter, beer, and salt.

Diet for Dandruff

Eat: Meat, fish, milk, whole grain cereals, cracked wheat bread, bananas, honey, vegetables, shellfish, and zinc tablets.

Avoid: Fried foods, spicy foods, and pork.

Diet for Diabetes

Eat: Soups, beef, lamb, poultry, eggs, skimmed milk, cheese, cauliflower, lettuce, sauerkraut, citrus fruits, raw tomatoes, almonds, spinach, and celery.

Avoid: Spicy foods, seafood, veal, pork, liver, kidneys, potatoes, yams, parsnips, carrots, peas, beans, corn asparagus, cabbage, radishes, winter squash, cereals, sugar, honey, all sweets, alcoholic beverages, and fish oils.

Diet for Dyspepsia

Eat: Beef Tea (see Chapter Five: Health Recipes), broiled steak, eggs, milk, grape juice, apple juice, orange juice, almonds, tomatoes, lettuce, potatoes, yogurt, waffles, papaya, pineapple juice, white bread, and tea.

Avoid: Fried foods, coarse vegetables, boiled dinners, veal, seafood, pork, ham, bacon, gravy, cheese sweets, wine, and coffee with cream or sugar.

Diet for Erysipelas

Eat: Arrowroot Water, Barley Water, Rice Water (see Chapter Five: Health Recipes), whole wheat bread without preservatives, farina, milk toast, orange juice, grape juice, and apple juice. Later on, when patient is better, add chicken, baked potatoes, spinach soufflé, rice, broiled lamb chops, lettuce, salads, and baked apples.

Avoid: Fried foods, fatty foods, cream, red meat, fish, shellfish, and sweets.

Diet for Eye Trouble

Eat: Carrot Tonic, Shaman Surprise (see Chapter Five: Health Recipes), carrot salad, carrot pudding, carrot cake, liver, cole slaw, cabbage, raw cabbage juice, okra, paprika, alfalfa sprouts, kelp, dandelion tea, crab, goose, duck, lamb, oysters, ham, heart, beef, veal, spinach, graham crackers, wheat germ, yeast, and sauerkraut.

Avoid: Fried foods and spicy foods.

Diet for Fingernails, Breaking

Eat: Liver, gelatin salads, carrots, broccoli, lamb, yeast, alfalfa sprouts, paprika, and eggs. For hangnail, add black currants, tomatoes, citrus fruit, and rose hips tea.

Avoid: Fried foods, pastries, and sweets.

Diet for Gallstones

Eat: Egg-Lemonade (see Chapter Five: Health Recipes), baked potatoes, lettuce, citrus fruits, white bread, orange juice, veal, lamb, radishes, raw asparagus, olive oil, buttermilk, parsley, grape juice, watermelon, cucumbers, gin, and lots of water between meals.

Avoid: Cereals, whole wheat bread, spinach, beans, carrots, egg yolks, fish, red meats, peaches, bananas, figs, dates, raisins, pastries, fried foods, hot breads, spicy foods, ice cream, and dairy products.

Diet for Gastritis

Eat: Lean meats, baked potatoes (with the skins), rice, cream soups, summer squash, spinach, peas, asparagus, bran, lettuce, grape juice, tomatoes, artichokes, and goat's milk.

Avoid: Pork, veal, seafood, fried foods, beans, cabbage, hot breads, left-overs, boiled dinners, spices, and sweets.

Diet for Gingivitis

Eat: Liver, celery, carrots, broccoli, blueberries, raspberries, asparagus, lima beans, whole grain products, green leafy vegetables, yogurt, salmon, low-fat milk, natural cheese, shellfish, fish, chicken, strawberries, apples, potatoes, yeast, oranges, peanuts, turnips, oats, and beans.

Avoid: Sugar, candy, sweets, raisins, dates, dried apricots, carbonated beverages containing sugar, beer, and wine.

Diet for Gland Trouble

Eat: Radishes, green vegetables, chicken, fish, lamb, baked potato peelings, and red wine with dark bread.

Avoid: Fried foods, pork, veal, boiled meat, spicy foods, and carbonated beverages.

Diet for Good Health

Eat: Whole grain cereals, salads, prunes, raisins, raw and steamed vegetables, yogurt, wheat germ, honey, baked potato peelings, soup, stew, fruit juice, dates, almonds, alfalfa sprouts, gelatin, lamb, wild game, chicken, fish, shellfish, lean beef, wild rice, herbs, sesame seeds, sunflower seeds, pumpkin seeds (especially for men), fruit, and tea. Black coffee, milk, eggs, licorice, and wine in moderation.

Avoid: Fried foods, fatty foods, charred meat, pork which is not well-done, synthetic foods, breads containing preservatives, heavy meats, sweets, processed cheese, and certain combinations of foods, such as fruits with vegetables, citrus fruit with milk, chicken with eggs, and pickles with ice cream.

Diet for Halitosis

Eat: Meat, fish, milk, whole grains, vegetables, alfalfa sprouts, parsley, tea, and black coffee.

Avoid: Garlic, onions, beer, and bourbon.

Diet for Heart Trouble

Eat: Gooseberries, spinach, oatmeal, lentil soup, baked potatoes, oysters Rockefeller, sesame seeds, hawthorn berries, fish, chicken, rice, skimmed milk, honey, bread, veal, fruit, vegetables, safflower and corn oil, carrot juice, and fresh pineapple.

Avoid: Hot breads, egg bread, sweetbreads, whole milk, duck, apples, goose, pork, kidneys, fatty meats, hot dogs, salami, bananas, sweets, potato chips, butter, cheese, coconut oil, olive oil, eggs (limit three per week), fried foods, non-dairy creamers, sour cream, and alcoholic beverages.

Diet for Hemorrhoids

Eat: Beef stroganoff, baked potatoes with the skins, raw carrots, cranberry juice, papaya juice, noodles, yogurt, sour cream, spinach, eggs, tomatoes, lamb, roast beef, broiled sirloin steak, fish, shellfish, white chicken meat, noodles, honey, brown rice, cracked wheat bread, sunflower seeds, nuts, oatmeal, cream of wheat, milk, herb teas, and raisin bran.

Avoid: Fried food, spicy food, pork, veal, boiled cabbage, rhubarb, cheese, sweets, barbecued spareribs, and alcoholic beverages.

Diet for Hepatitis

Eat: Meat, cheese, eggs, citrus fruit, lamb, fish, shellfish, chicken, spinach, tomatoes, strawberries, and rose hips tea.

Avoid: Fried food, starchy vegetables (potatoes, corn, yams, carrots, turnips, and rutabaga), sugar, honey, candy, pastries, hot bread, and spicy food.

Diet for Herpes Progenitalis

Eat: Beef, fish, chicken, pork, cheese, beans, milk, eggs, fruit, vegetables, shellfish, and yogurt.

Avoid: Raisins, nuts, oatmeal, brown rice, whole wheat bread, and peanut butter.

Diet for Housemaid's Knee

Eat: Green vegetables, tea, and milk.

Avoid: Meat, starchy foods, and pastries.

Diet for Hyperactivity

Eat: Magic Protein Potion (see Chapter Five: Health Recipes), shellfish, fish, chicken, homemade soup, garlic, lecithin, honey, curries, spinach, broccoli, salads, rice, yams, eggs, carrots, peas, celery, asparagus, natural cheese, bread without preservatives, and goat's milk.

Avoid: Sugar and all foods containing sugar, artificial coloring and flavoring, almonds, processed food containing additives, sulfites, apricots, bananas, berries, cherries, cloves, cucumbers, pickles, green peppers, nectarines, oranges, grapes, raisins, peaches, plums, prunes, tangerines, corn, tomatoes, white potatoes, tea, coffee, alcoholic beverages, beer, monosodium glutamate, aspirin, and chewing gum.

Diet for Jaundice

Eat: Egg-Lemonade (see Chapter Five: Health Recipes), chicken soup, and milk toast. Later on, when patient is better, add raw fruit, orange juice, summer squash and raw tomatoes.

Avoid: Fried foods, fats, sweets, eggs, pork, veal, duck, goose, bacon, potatoes, carrots, turnips, rutabaga, winter squash, pumpkin, and spicy foods.

Diet for Kidney Trouble

Eat: Hot cereals, watermelon, parsley, red wine with dark bread, asparagus, cranberry juice, fish, meat, green vegetables, citrus fruit, tomatoes, and liverwort tea.

Avoid: Dairy products, ice cream, and carbonated beverages.

Diet for Low Blood Pressure

Eat: Spinach, cabbage, oatmeal, dark bread, fruit, meat, eggs, milk, honey, vegetables, lemons, and garlic.

Diet for Malaria

Eat: For the first two days, every two hours: only the yolk of an egg shaken in a half a pint of Barley Water (see Chapter Five: Health Recipes). For the next three days: the white of an egg in a half pint of water, alternated with milk and Lime Water (see Chapter Five: Health Recipes) every two hours. For the next few days: milk, buttermilk, and fruit juice. Later on, the patient may eat Meigg's Food (see Chapter Five: Health Recipes), baked potatoes, oatmeal, brown bread, green vegetables, white fish, and white chicken.

Avoid: Meat, fried foods, spicy foods, and sweets.

Diet for Meningitis

Eat: Arrowroot Water, Egg-Lemonade, Jeneko Junket (see Chapter Five: Health Recipes), orange juice with the white of an egg, nut milk, dried coconut in milk, homemade chicken soup, lemonade, and tea.

Avoid: Fried foods, spicy foods, meat, coarse vegetables, sweets, and pastries.

Diet for Migraine Headache

Eat: Nganga Banana Shakes, Shamans Surprise (see Chapter Five: Health Recipes), avocados, oysters, lobster, chicken, custard, whole wheat bread, nuts, bacon, spinach, veal, broccoli, goose, duck, turkey, and asparagus.

Avoid: Pork, fried foods, spicy foods, candy, pastries, and cheese.

Diet for Muscular Dystrophy

Eat: Beef Tea, Magic Protein Potion (see Chapter Five: Health Recipes), mixed green salads, raw vegetables, spinach, oatmeal, wheat germ muffins, bananas, chicken, lamb, steamed vegetables, and white fish.

Avoid: Fried foods, spicy foods, pork, candy, or pastries.

Diet for Nervous Tension

Eat: Carrot Tonic (see Chapter Five: Health Recipes), mixed green salad, chicken salad, raw celery, fish, radishes, eggs, lettuce, raw carrots, asparagus, and milk.

Avoid: Fried foods, spicy foods, heavy meats, cabbage, beans, pastries, or coffee.

Diet for Nettle Rash

Eat: Lamb, mutton, goat, chicken, orange juice, grape juice, green vegetables, and brown bread.

Avoid: Strawberries, mashed or fried potatoes, cabbage, pork, veal, seafood, pears, plums, chocolate, tea, or coffee.

Diet for Neurasthenia

Eat: Bemba Bota, Nganga Banana Shakes, Whazi Wizi (see Chapter Five: Health Recipes), beets (almost daily), carrots, salads, raw vegetables, wheat germ muffins, steamed cabbage, cereals, bananas, pears, peas, liver, chicken, and white wine with meals.

Avoid: Polished rice, fried foods, raw cabbage, cole slaw, sweets, pastries, and spices.

Diet for Osteoporosis

Eat: Milk, cheese, almonds, walnuts, molasses, mustard greens, kale, lettuce, broccoli, brussels sprouts, okra, lima beans, parsley, peas, shrimp, clams, figs, whole wheat bread, string beans, wheat germ, and cereals.

Avoid: Fried foods, and sweets.

Diet for Paralysis

Eat: Jerusalem artichokes, Magic Protein Potion (see Chapter Five: Health Recipes), fish, shellfish, salads, raw vegetables, alfalfa sprouts, turnips, beets, carrots, parsnips, potatoes, and egg yolks.

Avoid: Egg whites, candy, spices, and fried foods.

Diet for Parkinson's Disease

Eat: Beets (not pickled) and beet tops twice a week, cabbage, eggs, carrots, raw and green vegetables, beans, corn, salads, liver, chicken, avocados, seafood, mushrooms, nuts, and bananas.

Avoid: Red meats, heavy meats, potatoes, yams, turnips, rutabaga, pork, popcorn, potato chips, fried foods, pastries, and sweets.

Diet for Pellagra

Eat: Voodoo Brew, Whazi Wizi (see Chapter Five: Health Recipes), calf liver, chicken, salmon, peanuts, milk, white fish, peanut butter, turkey, lamb, peas, beef, kale, and yeast.

Avoid: Fried foods, and pastries.

Diet for Peritonitis

Eat: Arrowroot Water (see Chapter Five: Health Recipes), homemade chicken soup, and milk at first; later add baked potatoes, white chicken meat, broiled lamb chops, roast lamb, boiled rice, baked apples, fruit juices, and red wine with dark bread.

Avoid: Fried foods, fats, mashed potatoes, pork, cabbage, or raw vegetables.

Diet for Plethora

Eat: Meat, chicken, eggs, milk, fruit, green vegetables, celery, tomatoes, beans, lentils, lettuce, and potatoes (in moderation).

Avoid: Turnips, rutabaga, carrots, parsnips, winter squash, pumpkin, and fruit and vegetables at the same meal.

Diet for Poisoning

Eat: At first only burnt toast with hot tea. When patient is better, he may have almonds, asparagus, bread, broccoli, custard, rice, eggs, lamb, peanut butter, honey, vinegar, whole grain cereals, milk, bananas, spinach, veal, wheat germ, and brewer's yeast.

Avoid: String beans, beans, cabbage, rhubarb, turnips, rutabaga, tuna, mussels, clams, or sword fish.

Diet for Prostatitis

Eat: Squash, tomatoes, rose hips tea, pumpkin pie, nuts, citrus fruit and juice, potatoes, spinach, strawberries, black currants, honey, royal jelly, and pumpkin seeds.

Avoid: Fried foods, spicy foods, pork, fats, and pastries.

Diet for Pyrosis

Eat: Magic Protein Potion (see Chapter Five: Health Recipes), baked potatoes, yams, lean meat, soups, broths, buttermilk, and dark bread.

Avoid: Pork, turkey, veal, or fatty meats.

Diet for Quinsy

Eat: Arrowroot Water, Rice Water, Toast Water (see Chapter Five: Health Recipes), milk, oatmeal, and ice cream.

Avoid: Any meat, poultry, fish, shellfish, or cheese until well.

Diet for Rheumatism

Eat: Chicken, squab, lamb, white fish, cereals, nuts, spinach, eggs, beets, fruit juices, stewed cucumbers, squash, brussels sprouts, string beans, artichokes, radishes, raw leafy vegetables, and soy beans.

Avoid: Fried foods, preserves, hot breads, red meat, duck, goose, turkey, pork, veal, potatoes, turnips, rutabaga, dairy products, monosodium glutamate, sweets, alcoholic and carbonated beverages.

Diet for Scarlet Fever

Eat: Boiled rice, cooked cereals, milk, ice cream, lemonade, fruit juices, catnip tea, and spearmint tea.

Avoid: Meat, fish, and shellfish until well.

Diet for Scars

Eat: Arrowroot Water, Corn Silk Tea (see Chapter Five: Health Recipes), Caesar salad, mixed green salad, seafood, raw vegetables, nuts, wheat germ muffins, chicken, and fruit.

Avoid: Fried foods, fats, and sweets.

Diet for Schizophrenia

Eat: Witch Doctor's Potion, Bemba Bota, Whazi Wizi, Zulu Brew (see Chapter Five: Health Recipes), Caesar salad, almonds, raw vegetables, raisins, dates, brewer's yeast, bacon, eggs, barley, beef, chicken, lamb, liver, heart, halibut, tuna, salmon, sardines, wheat germ muffins, bouillon, breads, honey, bran flakes, date nut cake, peanut butter, potato chips, rice, spaghetti, milk, and lecithin.

Avoid: Fried foods, fats, spicy foods, and sweets.

Diet for Scleroderma

Eat: Salads, raw vegetables, green vegetables, lean meats, white fish, white chicken meat, and homemade soups.

Avoid: Fatty meats; or rice, potatoes, bread, and spaghetti on the same day.

Diet for Scrofula

Eat: Beef, lamb, venison, chicken, eggs, milk, bread, rice, and farina.

Avoid: Too many vegetables and fruits.

Diet for Senility

Eat: Citrus fruit and juice, vegetables, black currants, beef, fish, shellfish, chicken, duck, sweet and sour pork, rice, baked potato peelings, sharks' fins, birds' nests, honey, royal jelly, pineapple, tomatoes, strawberries, noodles, milk, coffee, tea, rose hips tea, and lecithin.

Avoid: Fried foods, fats, spicy foods, and sweets.

Diet for Sexual Apathy

Eat: Raw oysters, oysters Rockefeller, lobster, clams, fish, Rocky Mountain oysters, whole wheat bread, asparagus, raw vegetables, avocados, grapes, passion fruit, lettuce, nuts, hearts of palm, spinach, watercress, carrot gelatin salad, chicken, Caesar salad, date nut cake, potato chips, graham crackers, pumpkin seeds, licorice, chocolate covered mints, champagne, wine, parfait d'amour, absinthe, ginseng tea, and wild game.

Avoid: Fried foods, crab meat, citrus fruit, and vinegar.

Diet for Skin Infections

Eat: Lamb, liver, veal, lean meat, bacon, chicken, goat, rice, mushrooms, whole grain cereals, bananas, pineapple, broccoli, asparagus, milk, spinach, graham crackers, cracked wheat bread, wheat germ, dates, rice, almonds, avocados, brewer's yeast, and Voodoo Brew (see Chapter Five: Health Recipes).

Avoid: Fried foods, sweets, strawberries, and citrus fruit.

Diet for Tonsillitis

Eat: Meigg's Food, Jeneko Junket, Nganga Banana Shakes, Magic Protein Potion, Shaman Surprise (see Chapter Five: Health Recipes), and coffee ice cream. When patient is better, add Bemba Bota, Voodoo Brew (see Chapter Five: Health Recipes), baked potatoes, raspberry gelatin, and rice.

Avoid: Meat, coarse vegetables, fried foods, spicy foods, fats, candy, or pastries.

Diet for Tympanites

Eat: Bemba Bota, Magic Protein Potion, Whazi Wizi, Witch Doctor's Potion, Papaya Tea, Zango Mango (see Chapter Five: Health Recipes), wheat germ muffins, and fresh fruit salad.

Avoid: Heavy meats, fried foods, spicy foods, cheese, sweets, blackberries, and pastries.

Diet for Typhoid Fever

Eat: Arrowroot Water, Rice Water, and Beef Tea (see Chapter Five: Health Recipes). When patient is better, add Magic Protein Potion, Voodoo Brew, Egg-Lemonade (see Chapter Five: Health Recipes), and orange juice. After apparent recovery, add Meigg's Food (see Chapter Five: Health Recipes), hot cereal, baked potatoes, and milk.

Diet for Ulcers

Eat: Hot cereals, creamed soups (not canned), milk, creamed dishes, white chicken meat, eggs, bread, cooked fresh vegetables, applesauce, and strained baby food.

Avoid: Raw fruits, raw or coarse vegetables, beets, fried foods, spices, lettuce, beer, or alcoholic beverages.

Diet for Varicose Veins

Eat: Hot cereals, raw vegetables, lettuce, spinach, citrus fruits, tomatoes, strawberries, and rose hips tea.

Diet for Warts

Eat: Shamans Surprise, Violet Wafers (see Chapter Five: Health Recipes), caviar, salads, raw vegetables, alfalfa sprouts, cole slaw, tomatoes, carrots, okra, parsley, paprika, honey, cabbage, beef, lamb, calf liver, chicken, yogurt, white bread, marmalade, eggs, milk, and rose water.

Avoid: Fried foods, and sweets.

Diet for Whooping Cough

Eat: Feed patient frequent small meals, and feed solid foods and liquids separately. At first, feed patient: orange juice, grape juice, apple juice, cranberry juice, grapefruit juice, chicken broth, turtle soup, and Toast Water (see Chapter Five: Health Recipes). Alternate this with baked potatoes, oatmeal, and gelatin.

Avoid: Fried foods, spicy foods, coarse fruits and vegetables, sweets, and pastries.

Diet for Wounds

Eat: Kiwi Pick-Me-Ups, Rookery Revivers (see Chapter Five: Health Recipes), rose hips tea, spinach, salads, raw vegetables, tomatoes, lamb, beef, chicken, calf liver, heart, rata wine, potato soup, brewer's yeast, strawberries, citrus fruit, oatmeal, bananas, honey, milk, and cracked wheat bread.

Avoid: Fried foods, spicy foods, and fats.

Diet to Gain Weight

Maoris in New Zealand take a picture of the person who wants to gain weight, draw an outline of a fuller figure around his image, and at the new moon have him color in the outline while chanting: "As the moon grows, so may I increase in size."

Eat: Kiwi Pick-Me-Ups, Rookery Revivers (see Chapter Five: Health Recipes), hot cereals, cream, honey, sugar, bananas, meat, fried eggs, bacon, ham, waffles, pancakes, French toast, butter, maple syrup, donuts, coffee cakes, hot breads, pastries, molasses, salt, peanut oil, peanuts, potatoes, yams, sour cream, pasta, potato chips, pretzels, wine, beer, malt, and soft drinks.

Avoid: Grapefruit, cottage cheese, and black coffee.

Diet to Lose Weight

Kahunas in Hawaii suggest eating 1 tsp of horseradish before each meal.

South African *sangomas* agree that one shouldn't eat more than 3 eggs per week, and can have a small serving of sweet potatoes, or a small baked potato every two weeks.

American Indian medicine men in Arizona suggest eating 1/2 grapefruit before lunch, and before dinner.

As with the diet to gain weight, take a picture of the person who wants to lose weight, tack it on the front of his refrigerator, and on the night of the full moon, have him snip off a piece of the excess weight from the picture while chanting: "As the moon wanes, so may I decrease in size."

The diet below is a well-balanced diet, so you can stay on it as long as you want, but consult your physician before beginning it. You can mix and match according to your tastes, but be sure you use sugar substitutes, salt substitutes, low-cal sweet margarine, and low-cal mayonnaise.

SUNDAY: *Breakfast*: Grapefruit, one poached egg on dry whole wheat toast, black coffee.
            Lunch: Pineapple boat (cubed fresh pineapple, oranges, papaya, and bananas in a pineapple shell with low-fat cottage cheese on top).
            Tea: Orange spice tea, and melba toast.
            Dinner: Roast turkey, string beans, and sweet potato balls.

MONDAY: *Breakfast*: Tomato juice, raisin bran with a banana, sugar substitute, and skim milk, black coffee.
            Tea: A raw carrot, tea with lemon or skim milk.

Dinner: Cracked crab, wheat germ muffin with low-cal cream cheese, steamed brussels sprouts.

TUESDAY: *Breakfast*: Grapefruit, one soft boiled egg, melba toast, black coffee.

Lunch: V-8 juice, spinach souffle.

Tea: Shrimp cocktail, tea with lemon or skim milk.

Dinner: Spaghetti, hearts of palm salad (without olives).

WEDNESDAY: *Breakfast*: Grapefruit, toasted English muffin with low-cal cream cheese, black coffee.

Lunch: Tomato juice, oysters Rockefeller.

Tea: Celery, tea with lemon or skim milk.

Dinner: Barbecued chicken, steamed carrots and pea pods.

THURSDAY: *Breakfast*: One slice of melon, raisin bran with skim milk and sugar substitute, black coffee.

Lunch: Grapefruit juice, low-cal cottage cheese, tomato, zucchini and alfalfa sprout salad, rye crisp.

Tea: Stuffed mushrooms, iced tea with lemon.

Dinner: Shish kebob, apricot pilaf, eggplant.

FRIDAY: *Breakfast*: Wheat germ muffin with low-cal margarine, black coffee, watermelon.

Lunch: Tuna salad, iced tea.

Tea: Watercress sandwich, tea with lemon.

Dinner: Broiled red snapper, wild rice, steamed broccoli.

SATURDAY: *Breakfast*: Fresh raspberries with plain yogurt (or skim milk), black coffee.
Lunch: Groundnut soup, skim milk.
Tea: Ceviche, iced tea.
Dinner: Calves' liver, herbed asparagus, stuffed baked potato.

SUNDAY: *Breakfast*: Grapefruit, one scrambled egg, black coffee.
Lunch: Minestrone soup, skim milk.
Tea: Shrimp remoulade, maté tea.
Dinner: Veal piccata, celery parmigiana, steamed cauliflower.

MONDAY: *Breakfast*: Orange juice, toasted English muffin with low-cal cream cheese, black coffee.
Lunch: Caesar salad, iced coffee.
Tea: Plain popcorn, tea.
Dinner: Rare roast beef with horseradish, brussels sprouts with water chestnuts, beets.

TUESDAY: *Breakfast*: Grapefruit, soft boiled egg, black coffee.
Lunch: Rare roast beef on toasted English muffin with horseradish, tea.
Tea: Trail mix, tea.
Dinner: Couscous, eggplant.

WEDNESDAY: *Breakfast*: Two fresh apricots, one soft boiled egg, black coffee.
Lunch: Pineapple and low-cal cottage cheese, melba toast.
Tea: Meatballs, tea.
Dinner: Bobotie, collard greens, black-eyed peas.

THURSDAY: *Breakfast*: One peach, raisin bran with skim milk, black coffee.

Lunch: Zulu Brew (see Chapter Five: Health Recipes), mixed green salad.

Tea: Crudité, tea.

Dinner: Stir fried turkey with oriental vegetables, steamed rice.

FRIDAY: *Breakfast*: Magic Protein Potion (see Chapter Five: Health Recipes), black coffee.

Lunch: Chicken soup, melba toast.

Tea: V-8 juice.

Dinner: Stuffed cabbage leaves.

SATURDAY: *Breakfast*: Grapefruit, one poached egg on dry toast, black coffee.

Lunch: Spinach salad, skim milk.

Tea: Hot clam canapes, tea.

Dinner: Teriyaki, pineapple beans, artichoke.

Other foods you can eat: Tuna packed in water, broiled white fish, Hungarian goulash and beef stroganoff (with yogurt), buffalo, noodles, kale, lentils, turnips, rutabaga, summer squash, venison, cucumbers, radishes, jicama, celery, onions, garlic, nectarines, apples (sparingly), plums, prunes, almonds, green salads with diet dressings, sukiyaki, sushi, Lomi Lomi, curries, pheasant, tofu, game hen, shrimp (or seafood) cocktail, oatmeal, lobster, roast lamb, broiled lamb chops, chili con carne, homemade soups, herb teas, and diet desserts.

Avoid: Wine, beer, liqueurs, champagne, caviar, whole milk, cream, sour cream, marshmallows, desserts, ice cream, candy, cookies, peanuts, pretzels, olives, pickles, fried foods, fats, gravy, potato chips, hot dogs, salty crackers, hamburgers, potato salad, macaroni salad, macaroni and cheese, avocados, turkey or chicken skin, hot breads, processed cheese, pork, fondue, tempura, donuts, coffee cake, butter, grapes, grape juice, mayonnaise (except low-cal), sugar, cocoa, bread (except low-cal), peanut butter (except no salt, low-cal), jams, jellies, tacos, burritos, tortillas, chili rellenos, pizza (except low-cal), waffles, pancakes, French toast, and malt.

Don't forget to exercise daily: Dancing, swimming, golf, tennis, jogging, aerobics, bowling, skiing, skating, bicycling, hiking, mountain climbing, walking, etc.

Don't get more than eight hours of sleep daily, and don't eat just before retiring.

Diet to Lower Cholesterol

Eat: Chicken Marco Polo, chicken curry, roast turkey, pheasant, venison, buffalo, lean beef and chicken saté with peanut sauce, fish (especially tuna, salmon, pampano en papillote, and trout), couscous, groundnut soup, watercress soup, cabbage, sweet and sour red cabbage, vegetables (especially carrots, broccoli, asparagus, cauliflower, brussels sprouts, winter squash, yams, and baked potatoes with their jackets), fruit (especially kiwi fruit, pineapple, bananas, prunes, blueberries, and apples), chili peppers, green salads, sesame seeds, yogurt, raisin bran, oat bran, oat bran muffins, oatmeal, skim milk (or not more than 1 percent fat), garbanzo beans, lima beans, kidney beans, cowpeas, egg whites, garlic, onions, corn oil, safflower oil, olive oil, vinegar, eggplant, grapefruit, lemons, limes, white wine in moderation, and herb tea (especially maté tea).

Avoid: Egg yolks, shrimp, sour cream, whole milk, poultry skin, chicken nuggets, bacon, ham, sausage, spareribs, steak, roast beef, pork chops, hot dogs, salami, bologna, duck, pancakes, French toast, fried potatoes, potato chips, peanut butter, butter, non-dairy creamer, coconut oil, palm oil, chili rellenos, gravy, lard, custard, fried foods, fatty foods, candy, ice cream, pastries, mayonnaise and cheese (except low cholesterol), too much caffeine, beer, colas, and diet drinks.

Gluten-Free Diet

Eat: Corn flakes, bread made without wheat, rye, or oat flour; fruit juice, honey, jelly, butter, margarine, carbonated beverages, cocoa, coffee, tea, custards, tapioca, gelatin, potatoes, refined rice, and hard sugar candy.

Avoid: Any foods containing wheat, rye, or oat products found in bread, cakes, cookies, and pastries. Any foods containing malt found in malted milk and beer, cream salad dressings, fruits with tough skins or seeds, vegetables with tough skins, fibers, seeds, nuts, chocolate, gravy, olives, pickles, potato chips, fried potatoes, sweet potatoes, yams, macaroni, noodles, spaghetti, pizza, cream soups, and popcorn.

High-Residue Diet

Eat: Fruits, cereals, eggs, bread, meat, potatoes, rice, nuts, spaghetti, coarse vegetables, chicken, fish, salads, wheat germ, milk, and at least six glasses of water daily between meals.

Liquid Diet

Drink: Shaman Surprise, Papaya Tea, Zulu Brew, Egg-Lemonade, Liver Tonic Mrewa, Magic Protein Potion, Nganga Banana Shakes, Carrot Tonic, Arrowroot Water, Barley Water, Lime Water, Rice Water, Toast Water, Witch Doctor's Potion, Voodoo Brew, Whazi Wizi,

Beef Tea, Zango Mango (see Chapter Five: Health Recipes), milk, and fruit juice.

Low-Residue Diet

Eat: Sugar, milk, eggs, lean meat (beef, lamb, or chicken) bran, gelatin, cooked white cereal, enriched white bread, ice cream, tapioca, eggnogs, rice pudding, plain cake, rice, custard, fruit juices, potato soup, spaghetti, butter, crackers, cottage or cream cheese, strained cooked fruits or vegetables, tea, and coffee.

Avoid: Raw fruit or vegetables, whole wheat cereal and bread, pork, veal, spices, fried or fatty foods, nuts, seeds, tomatoes, figs, and berries.

Low-Salt Diet

Eat: Garlic, onions, sour cream, yogurt, raisins, dates, nuts, rice, prunes, seeds, herbs, all fresh fruits and vegetables, fruit juices, salt-free soups and stews, salt-free bread, lemon juice, sweet margarine, unsalted popcorn, noodles, spaghetti, potatoes, yams, veal, beef, pork, lamb, chicken, turkey, duck, fish, eggs, gelatin, sherbet, ice cream, milk, tea, coffee, and alcoholic beverages and carbonated beverages (in moderation).

Avoid: Any foods containing salt, sea salt, baking powder, or baking soda, celery, olives, pickles, ketchup, bottled mustard, potato chips, tortillas, pretzels, pizza, waffles, pancakes, corn flakes, caviar, pickled herring, anchovies, sardines, canned tuna, shrimp, lobster, scallops, canned crab, cheese, cottage cheese, monosodium glutamate, soy sauce, steak sauce, baked beans, chili con carne, biscuits, pastries, donuts, puddings, crackers, graham crackers, kale, mustard greens, chocolate, cocoa, sauerkraut (and juice), corned beef; dried, spiced or chipped beef; bacon, ham, sausage, pastrami, bologna, salami, barbecued spareribs, frozen dinners; canned soups and vegetables, mayonnaise and peanut butter (unless labeled "no salt added"); salted nuts, frozen peas, frozen lima beans, and drinking water treated in a water softener.

CHAPTER FIVE

Health Recipes

*(Recipes utilized by traditional healers
in various lands for various purposes.)*

Arrowroot Water

1 tsp. arrowroot   1 pint water

Moisten arrowroot with cold water, smooth to a paste,
add 1 pint of boiling water and boil 5 minutes.

Barley Water

1 oz. barley   1 qts. water
Lemon rind   Sugar or honey

Wash pearl barley in cold water, boil 5 minutes and
drain. Pour on 2 qts. of boiling water and boil down to a
quart. Flavor with thinly cut lemon rind, and add sugar
or honey to taste.

Beef Tea

Round or rump beef   Water

Cut off all the fat from a piece of round or rump roast.
Put into a pint of cold water and soak for 2 hours. Simmer for 3 hours. Do not boil. Add cold water from time
to time. Press and strain.

Bemba Bota

1 cup cracked whole wheat	1 tbsp. soya flour
1 cup cracked rye	1 tbsp. brewer's yeast
1 cup rice bran	1 tbsp. bone meal

Mix and store ingredients in a glass jar. Cook 1 cup in 3 cups of boiling water for 3 minutes. Serve with honey and cream.

Carrot Tonic

2 raw carrots   1 cup milk

Blend together in an electric blender for 2 minutes.

Coconut Prune Cocktail

1½ cups prune juice	1 tsp. lime juice
1 cup orange juice	1 cup coconut water

Put all ingredients in an electric blender for 1 minute.

Corn Silk Tea

1 tsp. corn silk   1 cup boiling water

Chop up corn silk very fine, steep in boiling water for 1 hour. Cover until cool and strain.

Egg-Lemonade

2 lemons	1 pint boiling water
Whites of 2 eggs	Sugar to taste

Peel lemons twice, saving the yellow rind and throwing away the white layer. Place the sliced lemon and yellow peel in a quart jug with 2 lumps of sugar. Pour on the boiling water and stir. When cool, beat in the egg whites with a whisk. Strain through muslin and serve cold.

Jeneko Junket

½ pint milk   1 tsp. essence of pepsin

Heat milk, add pepsin, mix well, and pour into

custard cups. Let stand until firm, and sprinkle with nutmeg if desired.

Kava

Root of a pepper tree   Sugar
Water

In a special ceremony the Fiji islanders take the root of a pepper tree, boil it in water, and sweeten it with sugar.

Kiwi Pick-Me-Up

1/2 glass orange juice   1 tsp. honey
1/2 glass lemon juice   2 drops lemon extract

Mix ingredients together in a tall glass.

Lime Water

1 lump unslaked lime   2 quarts water

Into 2 quarts of water place a lump of unslaked lime the size of an egg. Stir thoroughly, and pour off the solution. Add fresh water, and keep covered.

Liver Tonic Mrewa

1 cup V-8 juice   1 slice raw white onion
1 tbsp. fresh parsley   A few sesame seeds
1 tbsp. raw liver   Salt and pepper to taste

Mix all ingredients in an electric blender for 1 minute. If liver is fresh, there should be no liver taste.

Magic Protein Potion

1 raw egg   1 tsp. safflower oil
8 oz. skimmed milk   4 tbsp. protein powder
1 tbsp. wheat germ   1/2 tsp. vanilla
1 saccharin tablet   Dash of nutmeg

Mix all ingredients in an electric blender for 1 minute. Sprinkle with nutmeg and drink at once.

Meigg's Food

1 tsp. gelatin (unflavored)   2 lumps sugar
1 level tsp. arrowroot   ½ cup cream

Soak gelatin in 6 tbsp. of cold water for ½ hour. Moisten arrowroot in 2 tbsp. cold water, and add ½ pint boiling water. Boil until clear, and add to gelatin. Stir until dissolved. Add lumps of sugar, cool, and add cream.

Mustard Plaster
(*For external use only*)

Dry mustard   White of 1 egg
Vinegar   1 tbsp. flour

Mix mustard with vinegar and boiling water, add the white of an egg and 1 tbsp. of flour. Mix to a thin paste, and spread on brown paper. Apply to the skin, and cover with a cloth.

Nganga Banana Shake

1 ripe banana   2 tsp. honey
2 tbsp. milk   1 glass unsweetened
1 tsp. brewer's yeast   pineapple juice

Mix all ingredients together in an electric blender for 30 seconds and drink at once.

Papaya Tea

1 papaya   1 lemon
2 tsp. honey   2 pints boiling water

Mash a papaya, seeds and all, add boiling water, and let stand 3 minutes, strain and reheat. Flavor with lemon and honey.

Rice Water

2 tbsp. rice   1 qt. boiling water
Salt to taste

Put rice in a granite saucepan with the boiling water. Simmer until the rice is soft, about 25 minutes, strain, and add salt to taste. May be served warm or cold.

Rookery Reviver

1 glass grapefruit juice   1 tsp. honey
3 drops lemon extract

Mix all ingredients together and drink at once.

Shaman Surprise

1 glass of milk   1 tbsp. Tiger's Milk
1 scoop vanilla ice cream 1 tbsp. wheat germ
1 tbsp. vanilla malt   1 jigger whiskey or French
1 dash of cinnamon   brandy

Mix together for 1 minute in an electric blender.

Toast Water

3 slices dark brown bread   1 qt. boiling water

Place toast in a pitcher with boiling water, cover closely, and strain when cool.

Violet Wafers

1 qt. sifted flour   1 tsp. salt
1 pint cold water   1 handful of bruised violet
                              petals

Mix all ingredients together, roll out thin, and cut into small cakes with a biscuit cutter. Place on a greased cookie sheet and bake 400° F. for 8 minutes.

Voodoo Brew

1 pint tomato juice   4 tbsp. brewer's yeast
1 pint sauerkraut juice   1 pinch caraway seeds

Mix all ingredients together in an electric blender for 1 minute, or mix with a wire whisk. Store in refrigerator, and shake well before drinking.

Whazi Wizi

1 pint V-8 juice   2 tbsp. brewer's yeast
1 pint yogurt   1 dash salt

Mix all ingredients together in an electric blender for 1 minute, or mix with a wire whisk. Store in refrigerator, and shake well before drinking.

Witch Doctor's Potion

1 ripe banana   1 cup milk
1 tsp. dried brewer's yeast   1 pinch caraway seeds
1 tsp. molasses   1 dash nutmeg

Mix all ingredients together in an electric blender for 1 minute. Sprinkle with nutmeg and drink immediately.

Zango Mango

1 mango   Juice of 1/2 lemon
1 tsp. honey   1 cup boiling water

Scoop out a mango, add honey and lemon juice. Mix in an electric blender for 1 minute with the boiling water.

Zulu Brew

1 glass sauerkraut juice   1 pinch caraway seeds
1 tsp. dried brewer's yeast   1 pinch poppy seeds
1 tsp. chopped parsley

Mix all ingredients together in an electric blender for 1 minute, or beat with a wire whisk. Drink at once.

CHAPTER SIX

Vitamins and Minerals

While witch doctors are successful in curing many psychosomatic illnesses by such native procedures as exorcising evil spirits, they realize that many diseases are caused by improper diets and that the deficiency of certain vitamins and minerals can cause serious physical symptoms, often leading to illness and death.

Below is a general list of vitamins and minerals, natural foods containing them, and symptoms caused by their deficiency.

Vitamins

Vitamin A: Found in: Polar bear liver, alfalfa sprouts, okra, dandelion greens, carrots, milk, paprika, parsley, kelp, watercress, cabbage, liver, and broccoli.

Deficiency causes: Indented lines in fingernails, night blindness, rough and dry skin, poor memory, irritability, confusion, insomnia, lowered resistance to infections, and acne.

Vitamin B_1 (Thiamine): Found in: Avocados, bananas, asparagus, bacon, yeast, Brazil nuts, cashew nuts, graham crackers, chicken, liver, lobster, oysters, whole wheat, wheat germ, beans, corn, mushrooms, apples, and onions.

Deficiency causes: Excessive sensitivity to sound, depression, shooting pains in the legs, nervous disorders, heart trouble, muscle degeneration, and beriberi.

Vitamin B₂ (Riboflavin): Found in: Almonds, asparagus, breads, broccoli, crab, goose, eggs, lamb, liver, oyster, peanut butter, heart, ham, graham crackers, beef, spinach, veal, wheat germ, and yeast.

Deficiency causes: Cracks in corners of the mouth, skin problems, burning sensations in feet and hands, sensitivity to light, anemia, and poor vision.

Vitamin B₃ (Niacin): Found in: Almonds, bacon, barley, beef, bouillon, bran flakes, breads, cereals, chicken, dates, lamb, mushrooms, halibut, heart, liver, peanut butter, potato chips, rice, salmon, sardines, spaghetti, tuna, and yeast.

Deficiency causes: Poor memory, confusion, poor blood circulation, cold feet, flushed face, sore and red tongue, tingling in fingers and toes, canker sores, bad breath, and depression.

Vitamin B₅ (Pantothenic Acid): Found in: milk, liver, kidneys, yeast, egg yolks, peas, bran, and molasses.

Deficiency causes: Skin abnormalities, dizzy spells, indigestion, painful and burning feet, fatigue, malaise, nausea, vomiting, headache, insomnia, and retarded growth in children.

Vitamin B₆ (Pyridoxine): Found in: Meat, fish, milk, whole grains, liver, brewer's yeast, and fresh vegetables.

Deficiency causes: Sore tongue, sore lips, dry mucous membrane, arthritis, and periodic pain in women.

Vitamin B₁₂ (Cyanocobalamin): Found in: Liver, beef, pork, kidneys, heart, eggs, milk, cheese, and brewer's yeast.

Deficiency causes: Loss of balance, tingling in fingers and toes, shooting pains, anemia, blood clotting, and periodic pain in women.

Folic acid: Found in: Liver, spinach, yeast, and kidneys.

Deficiency causes: Anemia.

Inositol: Found in: Fruits, nuts, whole grains, milk, meat, and yeast.

Deficiency causes: Falling hair.

Methionine: Found in: Meat, milk, eggs, fish, and cheese.

Deficiency causes: Cirrhosis of the liver.

Vitamin C (Ascorbic Acid): Found in: Citrus fruit, rose hips, black currants, strawberries, tomatoes, potatoes, spinach, green peppers, parsley, peas, cabbage, and asparagus.

Deficiency causes: Slow healing of wounds, senility, weakness, susceptibility to colds, bleeding gums, crevasses in the tongue, joint problems, hemorrhages, loose teeth, hardening of arteries, and scurvy.

Vitamin D: Found in: Effects of sunshine, cod liver oil, wheat germ, egg yolk, butter, cheddar cheese, liver, herring, cream, cod, salmon, sardines, shrimp, mackerel, and watercress.

Deficiency causes: Muscular weakness, tooth decay, retarded growth in children, and rickets.

Vitamin E: Found in: Lettuce, wheat germ, vegetable oils, eggs, and cereals.

Deficiency causes: Senility, sterility, impotence, muscular dystrophy, and heart trouble.

Vitamin F: Found in: Barley, coconut, peanuts, corn, oats, olives, rice, rye, and sunflower seeds.

Deficiency causes; Skin disorders.

Vitamin K: Found in: Cabbage, cauliflower, tomatoes, egg yolks, spinach, alfalfa sprouts, and soybeans.

Deficiency causes: Hemorrhages and blood clots.

Vitamin P: Found in: Citrus fruit, honey, black currants, lemon peel, and grapes.

Deficiency causes: Susceptibility to infections and colds, hypertension, and purplish spots on the skin.

Vitamin U: Found in: Raw cabbage and alfalfa sprouts.

Deficiency causes: Constipation, vomiting, stomach pains, and peptic ulcers.

Minerals

Calcium: Found in: Milk, cheese, almonds, Brazil nuts, hazelmuts, maple syrup, molasses, mustard greens, okra, olives, peas, parsley, prunes, raisins, walnuts, watercress, shrimp, figs, clams, broccoli, whole wheat bread, string beans, lima beans, collards, lentil, and kale.

Deficiency causes: Pains in the joints, cramps, numbness in the arms and legs, broken fingernails, tooth decay, softening of the bones, and heart trouble.

Iodine: Found in: Fish, shellfish, iodized salt, seaweed, and kelp.

Deficiency causes: Thyroid trouble, goiter, lack of energy, and retarded growth in children.

Iron: Found in: Almonds, apricots, beef, Brazil nuts, whole wheat bread, chard, bouillon, egg yolks, hazelnuts, liver, kidneys, heart, lamb, molasses, oat-meal,oysters, parsley, prunes, peaches, raisins, rice, soybeans, turkey, tongue, turnip greens, wheat germ, and yeast.

Deficiency causes: Anemia, weakness, fatigue, irritablitiy, and brittle nails.

Magnesium: Found in: Watermelon, turnips, carrots, kelp, cereal, rutabagas, raspberries, raw spinach, nuts, wheat germ, and whole grain bread.

Deficiency causes: Poor memory, confusion, mental problems, and heart trouble.

Potassium: Found in: Grapes, cranberries, strawberries, bananas, raspberries, paprika, turnips, watercress, soybeans, baked potato skins, lamb, molasses, and watermelon.

Deficiencies causes: Muscular weakness, paralysis, and respiratory trouble.

Zinc: Found in: Red meat and shellfish.

Deficiency causes: Loss of smell and taste, loss of hair, failure of wounds to heal, arthritis, retarded growth in children, dandruff, athlete's foot, and body odor.

In many cases witch doctors and other traditional healers may prescribe vitamins and minerals in pill or capsule form. Vitamin E capsules, for example, when applied externally to burns, have a healing effect and prevent scarring. In the Middle East, shamans have discovered that those who take vitamin B_1 tablets seem to repel sandflies and mosquitoes. It apparently produces a scent on their skin the insects avoid.

CHAPTER SEVEN

Traditional Therapeutic Properties of Herbs

Witch doctors, as other traditional healers, use herbs in tea and poultices, often in combination with other herbs. Their administration is usually accompanied by rituals and incantations.

For general interest only, and not in any way as a prescription, many common herbs they use are listed below with their alleged therapeutic applications.

Don't attempt to use these herbs without medical guidance, as to appropriateness, method of preparation and dosage—none of this information is given here. Remember that some herbs may be poisonous whether so indicated here or not.

In any case, self diagnosis and treatment should be avoided. If you need medical help, consult a qualified health practitioner.

Abscess root: Pleurisy, and respiratory disorders.
Acacia: Mouthwash.
Aconite (wolf's bane, leopard's bane, or monkshood): Poisonous. For milk leg, and peritonitis.

Agrimony: Blood purifier, snake bite, and cauterization of wounds.

Alder: Blood circulation, diarrhea, and hemorrhages.

All-Heal: Convulsions, cramps, and digestive disorders.

Allspice: Flatulence.

Aloe Vera: Burns, radiation burns, and scorpion stings.

Amadou: Hemorrhages.

Amaranth (prince's feather, pilewort, lady bleeding, red cock's comb): Menorrhagia, and bleeding hemorrhoids.

Anemone: Amenorrhea, and inflammation of the eyelids.

Angelica: Colds, and pneumonia.

Anise: Constipation, indigestion, liver disorders, and colic.

Arnica: Poisonous. Skin trouble, neuralgia, circulation disorders, and brain concussion.

Asafetida: Mononucleosis, nervous tension, and prevention of disease.

Ashberries: Dysmenorrhea.

Ave-grace: Insect bites.

Avena: Dysentery.

Ayawasca (a South American herb): Hangovers.

Balm: Fevers.

Balmgilead: Hemorrhoids.

Basil: Nervous tension, and rheumatism.

Bayberry: General tonic.

Bay leaves: Cramps, and digestive disorders.

Bearberry: Indigestion, and tonic.

Bearsfoot: Liver, spleen disorders, and white swelling.

Beech: Wounds, and ulcers.

Belladonna (deadly nightshade): A narcotic, poisonous. For diverticulitis, and eye examinations.

Benne: Stomach trouble.

Bilberry: Asthma.

Birch leaves: Arthritis.

Birthwort: Respiratory disorders.

Bistort: Urinary diseases, sore mouth, and sore gums.

Biting Stonecrop: Ulcers.

Bitterroot: Sore throat.

Bittersweet: Skin trouble, jaundice, and venereal disease. Poisonous.

Blackberries: Diarrhea, and dysentery.

Black Cohosh: Dysmenorrhea, and lumbago.

Black Currant: Dysentery.

Black Haw: Female disorders.

Black Root: Blood disorders.

Bladder Wrack: Metabolic disorders, and goiter.

Blessed Thistle: Antidote for some poisons.

Bloodroot: Coughs, colds, and bronchitis. Poisonous.

Blueberries: Multiple sclerosis.

Blue Flag: Ulcers, and tumors.

Blue Mallow: Respiratory disorders.

Boldo: Gallbladder problems.

Boneset: Skin ailments, and malaria.

Borage: Pulmonary disorders.

Brooklime: Blood disorders.

Broomcorn: Bladder, and kidney problems.

Bryony: Rheumatism.

Bougainvillea: Laryngitis.

Buckwheat: Headache, stomachache, high blood pressure, and bronchitis.

Bugleweed: Hemoptysis.

Burdock: Boils, and cysts.

Burnet: Sour stomach.

Burra: Urinary disorders.

Butcher's-Broom: Female problems.

Butea Monsperma: Birth control.

Butterbur: Asthma.

Calamus (sweet flag): Colic, dyspepsia, and flatulence. May be carcinogenic.

Calotropia: Elephantiasis, and skin eruptions.

Camomile: Female disorders, hangovers, and bullet wounds.

Camphor: Colds, neuralgia, blackheads, blisters, chest pains, strains, and skin eruptions.

Caraway seeds: Flatulence, colic, and a diuretic.

Caroba: Nervous tension.

Cassia: Laxative.

Castor Oil: Warts, corns, and a laxative.

Catnip: Spider bites, colds, pain reliever, acidity, and measles.

Cayenne (red pepper): Liniments, and eye trouble.

Centaury: Tonic, and stimulant.

Chaparral: Cancer.

Cherry juice: Gout, and a blood tonic.

Chervil: Swellings.

Chestnut leaves: Whooping cough.

Chicory: A tonic, and a laxative.

Chickweed: Kidney ailments.

Chokecherry: Diarrhea, and nervous tension.

Cicely: Stomach trouble.

Cinchona: Fever, and malaria.

Cinnamon: Morning sickness, diarrhea, gargle, and poliomyelitis.

Cloves: Toothache, nausea, and Bright's disease.

Club Moss: Urinary disorders.

Coast Tarweed: A remedy for poison oak and poison ivy.

Colombo: Rheumatism, and tuberculosis.

Columbine: Secretions, arthritis, venereal disease, and dizziness.

Comfrey: Tumors, cancer, emphysema, orchitis, and osteomyelitis.

Copaiba: Catarrh.

Coriander: Stomach tonic.

Cornflower: Eye disorders.

Corn Silk: Kidney disorders.

Cornsmut: Hemorrhages, and female disorders.

Cranberries: Kidney trouble, scarlet fever, erysipelas, and hemorrhoids.

Crawley: Pleurisy.

Cuckoopint: Sore throat.

Cup of Gold: Strep throat.

Cup Plant: Disorders of the internal organs.

Dandelion: Yaws, and hepatitis.

Desert tea: Gonorrhea.

Dill: Nausea, gastritis, indigestion, and croup.

Dog Rose: Nutritional supplement.

Dogwood: Dropsy, and diarrhea.

Dulce: Colds, and catarrh.

Dwale: Tumors, and cancer.

Elecampane: Skin cleanser, stomach trouble, and sluggish liver.

Embelia: Rheumatism.

Ephedra: Hay fever, and asthma.

Erynogo: Female disorders.

Eucalyptus: Fevers, antiseptic, liniment, backache, and respiratory disorders.

Euphorobia: Respiratory disorders.

Eyebright: Eye trouble.

Fennel: Diuretic, and laxative.

Five Leaf Grass: Diarrhea, and dysentery.

Flaxseed: Gonorrhea, jaundice, measles, metritis, and carbuncles.

Fleabane: Insect repellent for fleas.

Fleawort: Mouth ailments.

Fluellin: Bleeding, and purpura.

Fenugreek: Colds, and pneumonia.

Fo-ti-Tieng: Digestion, longevity, sterility, impotence, and general tonic.

Foxglove (digitalis): Heart trouble. Poisonous.

Gardenia (for external use only): Open sores.

Garlic: Hypertension, and many other uses.

Gelsemium: Nervous disorders.

Gentian: Hemorrhoids, and female disorders.

Geranium root: Hemorrhages, and summer complaint.

Ginger: Cramps, meningitis, and nausea.

Ginseng root: Senility, impotency, longevity, sterility, stimulant, and general tonic.

Goldenseal: Quinsy, morning sickness, acne, pyorrhea, a general tonic, and a laxative.

Gotu Kola (from India): A blood purifier, diuretic, tonic aphrodisiac, and stimulant.

Goutwort: Gout, and sciatica.

Groelandica: Alcoholism.

Hartstongue: Internal organs.

Hawthorn berries: Angina pectoris.

Heal-All: Cramps, digestive disorders, and convulsions.

Hibiscus flowers: Constipation, and catarrh.

Hollyhock: Throat ailments.

Holy Thistle: Fevers, and colds.

Hooweeyo (a South American herb): Burns.

Hops: Indigestion, and anemia.

Horehound: Sore throats, and open sores.

Horse Chestnut: Hemorrhoids, and rheumatism. Poisonous.

Horseradish: High blood pressure, hoarseness, and dysmenorrhea.

Horsetail (shave grass): Female disorders, and abscesses.

Huckleberry leaves: Diarrhea.

Iceland Moss: Respiratory ailments.

Ivy: Ulcers, sores, and abscesses.

Indian Hemp root: Palsy, and chorea.

Indian Snakeroot (rauwolfia): Poisonous. Snake bite, colitis, nervous and mental disorders.

Jamborandi: Asthma, and spotted fever.

Jewelweed: Hemorrhoids, and athlete's foot.

Juniper berries: A diuretic, and laxative.

Kelp: Goiter.

Knapweed: Mouth disorders, and nosebleed.

Lady's Bedstraw: Urinary disorders.

Lady's Slippers: Neuralgia.

Larkspur: Lice.

Lavender: Nervous disorders.

Lemon Grass: Kidney problems.

Lilac leaves: Malaria.

Licorice root: Constipation, menopause, and Addison's disease.

Linden flowers: Indigestion.

Loco Weed: Sore throat, and swellings. Poisonous.

Lotus root: Sinus trouble.

Lungwort: Lung ailments.

Madonna Lily: Female disorders.

Magnolia bark: Fever, dyspepsia, dysentery, erysipelas, malaria, and a tea to quit smoking.

Mahogany bark: Colds, and lung trouble.

Mandrake: Narcotic, a stimulant, a tonic, an aphrodisiac, and an anesthetic. Poisonous.

Manna: A laxative.

Marigold: Fevers, heart ailments, and skin trouble.

Marjoram: Colds, measles, headaches, and acidity.

Marshmallow root: Hematuria, and iritis.

Masterwort: Amenorrhea, asthma, palsy, dropsy, and apoplexy.

Maté (a South American herb): Stimulant and tonic.

Meadowsweet: Diarrhea.

Monsonia: Digestive disorders.

Motherwort: Stimulant and tonic.

Mountain Laurel: Mouth disorders.

Mugwort: Pain, and as an amulet for sterility. Poisonous.

Mullein leaves: Digestive disorders, coughs, colds, diarrhea, and hemorrhoids.

Mustard: Gastritis, and as a plaster for chest colds, and apoplexy.

Nasturtium leaves: As a poultice for ringworm.

Nettle tea: Backache, diarrhea, dysentery, hemorrhages, colds, fever, and influenza.

Oat Straw tea: Insomnia.

Orange Blossom tea: Yellow fever.

Oregano: Leukorrhea.

Papaya: Corns, digestive ailments, hemorrhoids, and backache.

Paprika: Post nasal drip, and sinus trouble.

Parsley: Halitosis, dropsy, and a diuretic.

Passion Flower: Typhoid fever, and colitis. Is a sedative, a nervine, and an anti-spasmodic.

Peach leaves: Gastric disorders, and hematuria.

Pennyroyal: Colic, leprosy, gout, convulsions, and insect repellent.

Peony: Epilepsy.

Pepper: Neuralgia.

Peppermint: Digestive disorders, nausea, and painter's colic.

Periperi (a South American herb): Birth control.

Periwinkle: Hodgkin's disease. Poisonous.

Peruvian Bark: Malaria, and jaundice.

Peyote: A strong narcotic. A painkiller, or anesthetic.

Pine: Scars, bronchitis, coughs, sore throat, and respiratory ailments.

Pitcher Plant: Stomach ailments.

Plantain: Catalepsy, snake bite, syphilis, wounds, bleeding, and spotted fever.

Pleurisy root: Pleurisy, and spotted fever.

Poke root: Ulcers, and ringworm.

Poplar: Analgesic, fevers, malaria, and skin trouble.

Pot Barley: Diarrhea.
Primrose: Wounds, and bleeding.
Psylla: Digestive disorders.
Pulsatilla: Female disorders.
Pumpkin seeds: Prostate trouble, metritis, and worms.
Purslane: Respiratory ailments.
Quassia: Fevers, dyspepsia, rheumatism, and worms.
Queen of the Meadow: Rheumatism, lame back, and dropsy.
Ragwort: Female trouble.
Raspberries: Influenza, colds, fevers, and childbirth.
Red Clover: Colds, respiratory ailments, and high blood pressure.
Rose Hips: Colds, scurvy, and senility.
Rosemary: Bronchitis, asthma, and arthritis.
Saffron: Female disorders.
Sage: Eye trouble, heat prostration, mercurial disease, and mumps.
Sangre de Grado (a South American herb): Bleeding.
Sarsaparilla: Blood disorders, and psoriasis.
Sassafras: A blood purifier and tonic. For measles, shingles, hives, mononucleosis, nettle rash, and boils.
Saw Palmetto: Glandular disorders.
Self-Heal: Bleeding wounds.
Senna: Constipation, and tympanitis.
Sesame seeds: Soldier's heart, and other heart ailments.
Shepherd's Purse: Hemorrhages, and internal hemorrhoids.
Silverweed: Skin trouble.
Skullcap: Nervous disorders, insomnia, and headache.
Slippery Elm: Wounds, skin trouble, scrofula, and bunions.
Snowberries: Hernia.
Solomon's Seal: Bone strengthener.
Sorrel: Tumors and swellings.
Southernwood: Antidote for some poisons.

Spearmint: Heart trouble, metritis, smallpox, and painter's colic.

Speedwell: Hyperthryroidism, and goiter.

Stickwort: Tumors, and ulcers.

Stramonium (jimson weed): Poisonous. Asthma, enteritis, rat-bite fever, milk leg, and other ailments.

Strawberries: For removing tartar on teeth.

Summer Savory: Ear trouble.

Sunflower seeds: Arthritis, and respiratory ailments.

Tamarind: Laxative, biliousness, and fever.

Tansy: Blood disorders, and amenorrhea.

Taro root: As a poultice for cysts, tumors, and toxicity.

Thyme: Bronchitis and coughs.

Tobacco: Colic, ear trouble, tetanus, and nervous tension.

Turmeric: Skin problems, asthma, bronchitis, fever, and a diuretic.

Uva Ursi: Bright's disease, kidney trouble, gonorrhea, and hemorrhoids.

Valerian: Nervous disorders, and insomnia.

Vanilla Pods: Neurasthenia, and flatulence.

Vervain: Stimulant.

Violet flowers: Cancer, tumors, and ulcers.

Wahoo: Liver disorders. Poisonous.

Walnut leaves: Skin disorders, scrofula, and insect repellent.

Watercress: Anemia, coughs, heart trouble, and a diuretic.

Watermelon seeds: Dropsy, heart ailments, high blood pressure, kidney trouble, gonorrhea, nephritis, and nephrosis.

Wheatgrass: Arthritis, and neurasthenia.

White Clover: Boils, ulcers, and skin diseases.

White Oak bark: Goiter, and leukorrhea.

White Oregon Grape: Leukorrhea, liver and kidney problems.

White Pond Lily: Stomach disorders, and ulceration of the womb.

White Willow: Stomach disorders, heartburn, and fever.

Wild Indigo: Paratyphoid fever, and benign breast tumors.

Wild Yams (dioscorea): A root from Mexico, poisonous. For appendicitis, arthritis, asthma, burns, eye and skin infections, and sterility.

Willow bark: Arthritis, headache, and general pain reliever.

Wintergreen: Cataracts, rheumatism, and mouthwash.

Witch Hazel: A wash for tumors, inflammations, bed-sores, sore eyes, and headache.

Wood Betony: Stomach trouble, headache, palsy, and dropsy.

Wood Sage: Bleeding wounds, and cold sores.

Wormwood: Impotency. Poisonous.

Woundwort: Bleeding wounds.

Xanthium: Rabies.

Yarrow: Colds, respiratory diseases, hemorrhages, and hemorrhoids.

Yellow Dock: Cysts, and skin ailments.

Yellow Pond Lily: Nymphomania.

Yerba de la Raya (a Mexican herb): Stingray stings.

Yerba Santa: Bronchitis, colds, venereal diseases, coughs, and stomach trouble.

Bibliography

Adam, Lt. Col. James M. *A Traveller's Guide to Health*, Hodder and Stoughton Ltd., London, England, 1966.

Albertus Magnus. *Egyptian Secrets*, U.S.A. N.p.n.d.

American National Red Cross. *Standard First Aid and Personal Safety*, Doubleday and Co., Garden City, N.Y., 1973.

Baxter, Richard. *The Certainty of the Worlds of Spirits*, London, England, 1691.

Bauer, W. W., M.D. *Potions, Remedies, and Old Wive's Tales*, Garden City, N.Y. 1969.

Bolton, Brett. *Edgar Cayce Speaks*, Avon Books, New York, 1969.

Brand, John. *Popular Antiquities of Great Britain*, London, England, 1905.

Chase, A. W., M.D. *Dr. Chase's Receipt Book*, F. B. Dickerson and Co., Detroit, Mich., 1889.

Conn, Howard F., M.D. *Current Therapy*, W. B. Saunders Co., Philadelphia, Pa., 1950.

Dalyell, John. *The Darker Superstitions of Scotland*, Edinburgh, Scotland, 1834.

Davis, Adelle. *Let's Get Well*, Harcourt, New York, 1965.

Fishbein, Morris, M.D. *Modern Home Medical Adviser*, Doubleday and Co., Inc., Garden City, N.Y., 1949.

Gelfand, Michael. *Witch Doctor*, Harvill Press, London, England, 1964.

Grendon, Felix. *The Anglo Saxon Charms*, New York, 1901.

197

Harris, Ben Charles. *Kitchen Medicines*, Barre Publishers, New York, 1968.

Jarvis, D. C., M.D. *Folk Medicine*, W. H. Allen and Co., London, England, 1960.

King-Richardson Co. *The Cottage Physician*, King-Richardson Co., Massachusetts, 1893.

Kourennoff, Paul. *Russian Folk Medicine*, Pyramid Books, New York, 1971.

Kreig, Margaret. *Green Medicine*, Rand McNally Co., New York, 1964.

Kuhne, Paul, M.D. *Home Medical Encyclopedia*, Fawcett Publications, Inc., Connecticut, 1960.

Leland, Charles. *Gypsy Sorcery and Fortune Telling*, London, England, 1891.

Maxwell, Nicole. *The Witch Doctor's Apprentice*, Houghton Mifflin Co., Boston, Mass. 1961.

Merck and Co., Inc. *The Merck Manual*, Merck & Co., Inc., New Jersey, 1976.

Paulson, Kathryn. *Magic and Witchcraft*, The New American Library, New York, 1970.

Schifferes, Justud J., Ph.D. *The Family Medical Encyclopedia*. Little, Brown and Co., Boston, 1959.

Stone, Robert B., Ph.D., Stone, Lola. *Hawaiian and Polynesian Miracle Health Secrets*, Parker Publishing Co., New York, 1980.

Winter, Evelyne. *Mexico's Ancient and Native Remedies*, Guadalajara, Mexico, 1969.

Sorcerers Around the World

Guam: *Surahos* (male), and *surahas* (female)

Hawaii: *Kahunas*

Mexico and South America: *Brujos* (male), *brujas* (female) and *curanderos* (healers)

Portugal and Brazil: *Bruxas*

The United States: American Indian medicine men, and Vermont folk practitioners

South Africa: *Sangomas* (full-fledged witch doctors or sorcerers), and *Twasas* (apprentice witch doctors)

Senegal: *Marabouts*

West Africa (Ivory Coast, Togo, Benin): Ju-ju men

Uganda, Zimbabwe, Gabon, Ghana: *Ngangas*

France and Canada: *Sorciéres* (sorcerers), *guerisseurs* (healers)

The Sudan: *Abinzas*

India: Gurus, swamis, and yogis

Ireland: Druid magis

Kenya: *Murdumugas*

Indonesia: *Dukans*

Tibet: *Naljorpas*

Borneo: *Bomohs*

Thailand: *Krous*

Turkey: *Hodjis* (male), *Hodjas* (female)

Russia, and Eastern Europe: Shamans (male), shamankas (female)

Germany: *Hexes*

Yap: *Tumerangs*

Haiti: *Houngans* and voodootherapists

Italy: *Stregas*

Index